Minnie Ward Patterson

Pebbles From Old Pathways

ISBN/EAN: 9783337057084

Printed in Europe, USA, Canada, Australia, Japan

Cover: Foto ©Thomas Meinert / pixelio.de

More available books at **www.hansebooks.com**

Minnie Ward Patterson

Pebbles From Old Pathways

Pebbles from Old Pathways.

BY

MINNIE WARD PATTERSON.

CHICAGO:

C. J. BURROUGHS & CO., PRINTERS, 198 CLARK ST.

1875.

Friends of Lang Syne:

Pursuant to your many requests I have at length put these poems into a book. Its errors and deficiencies, I know you will pardon, because of the friendship you bear me, and the old times recalled by its pages.

As to the great world, I have heard it is full of willing surgeons, (some of whom may be quacks,) into whose hands the fledgeling must fall. If its eyes do not match, they will extract them; if its limbs are unequal, they will amputate them; if its blood is imperfect, they will remove it; and, if its plumage offend, not a pin-feather will they allow to remain.

How long it will take to complete the operation, I know not; but, when the remains are brought to my view, and I gaze, through tears, on the fragments of that little crow, (which never pretended to be exactly white, nor altogether symmetrical,) when I think how hard I scratched for the worms which gave it what little roundness it possessed, and remember the maternal delusion that saw beauty in its form and gait, and heard music in its systematic cawings, I beg your sympathy, and somewhat expect it; for some of you have learned by similar experience, both the value and method of suitable commiseration. At the cremation—the last sad duty to the dissected bird—all are respectfully invited to assist

THE AUTHOR.

PROEM.

Weary, the traveler turns his feet towards the home
   . of his childhood—
  Golden its portals gleam, like a fane of enchanted
    glow;
Memory's sacred altar flushes the waste of its
    wildwood,
  Burning his present joys to brighten the long ago.

What though the Indies pour their wealth in his
    willing bosom?—
  Little and light the boon, as the slow years onward
    flow;
Little and light, to one who treasures a withered
    blossom,
  Plucked by some loving hand, in the beautiful
    long ago.

Amulets, quaint and fair, he bears on his desert
     roaming—
  Rings and ringlets of gold, and letters that dearer
     grow:
Sweet, to him, the mystic strains they summon at
     gloaming—
  Echoes of voices loved in the wonderful long ago.

Each has his treasures old—reminders of early
     rambles,
  Gathered with merry hands from the paths we
     used to know;
Yours may be gems and flowers—mine are but
     pebbles and brambles,
  Yet may you hold them dear, for the sake of the
     long ago.

LEFT FOR DEAD.

The battle is over, 'tis quiet again;
   In the chill, and the blood, and the damp,
They have left me for dead, so faint was my moan,
   And they've carried the wounded to camp.
In the morning, they'll come and bury us boys,
   And they'll never know of the strife
Of this struggling soul, and this dying tongue,
   For a day or two more of life.

This cloud of smoke smothers me, where I lie,
   And the campfires look red through the haze;
The boys are rejoicing,—I hear what they say,
   As they gather around the blaze.
Yes, "the war *is* now past"—from the very first fight,.
   I have carried my musket, till now:—
In Heav'n I'll be glad that I died for the right,
   Though no laurels encircle my brow!

I wish I but knew if their general FELL,
  When the ranks of the enemy broke;
For, when I took aim, there was haze in my eyes,
  And he waved, like a ghost, in the smoke.
Well, death must come some time, and so let it come,
  But I hope they will let Mary know
That the one she most honored was strong till the
    last—
  That I died *with my face to the foe*.

I've no fault to find in the matter, but yet,
  Though I'm proud to die just as I am,
It would seem nearer right could I feel Katie's touch,
  Or the kiss of my dear little Sam.
I know they remember me now, but I hope,
  To remember me longer, they'll try;
No matter—they'll find me at roll call, I know—
  Till then—home and dear ones—good-bye!

LINES UPON VISITING MY NATIVE VILLIAGE.*

Dear old village! am I wand'ring
   Once again your grassy way?
Do I tread the quiet valleys,
   Where, a child, I used to play?
Darling sister, 'tis like dreaming—
   Holding thus your hand in mine;
And the old love, on me beaming,—
   Thrills me like a gleam divine!

Oft, in slumber, comes a vision
   Of the happy long-ago;
But it always flees at morning,
   And I fear this may do so,
While we linger near the cottage
   Where our precious mother died;
And old mem'ries, thronging 'round us,
   Flit, like ghosts, on every side.

*Niles, Mich.

I can see her at the window,
   As I saw her when a child,
As she glanced, from work or reading,
   At our merry sport, and smiled:
Or, when ruder grew our gladness,
   As she turned on us her eyes,
With a sadness that rebuked us,
   Like a whisper from the skies.

Cruel hands have lopped the branches
   That o'erhung our humble door;
Yet the robins love to linger .
   Where they sang, in days before.
It may be the love of old times
   Clings to *them* as well as *me;*
And, though gone, they love to warble
   Near *where stood* their native tree.

Oh! how little did I prize thee,
   Angel mother, while on earth!
But, in long, sad years without thee,
   I have partly learned thy worth.

What would I not give to tell thee
  All the heart-aches of those years,
And indulge, upon thy bosom,
  In the luxury of tears!

Can it be—my gentle mother—
  That this lone, neglected mound,
Where the grass, in wildness trailing,
  Shuts the sunlight from the ground;
And, with billows never broken,
  Hides thy dwelling—can it be
That the children thou hast cherished
  Make no fairer couch for thee!

Hard it is to gaze upon it,
  As the all that I may see;
But 'tis sweet to know one angel
  Loving waits in Heav'n for me.
Tell me not, cold-hearted skeptic,
  That the dead are gone for aye:—
I have felt her soft arms fold me,
  As I knelt to weep and pray.

Felt the air of Heaven stealing
   O'er my earthly, tear-stained cheek,
As she nightly hovered o'er me,
   Words of peace and hope to speak :—
Waked to hear the words of music
   Ling'ring still, as when I slept—.
Known that angels were around me,
   And for very gladness wept!

Farewell! to thy low bed, mother;
   Though I know 'tis nought of thee,
Yet I would that ever near it,
   While on earth, my home might be.
For, when sorrows thicken 'round me,
   It would seem a wond'rous rest,
Could I seek thy lonely pillow—
   Weep them out upon thy breast!

Farewell! gentle, patient sister,
   Who, through every good and ill,
Unkind word of mine, and action,
   Faithful art, and patient still.

These few days with thee have shown me
    What an earnest soul can be;
And how much my own must conquer,
    Ere I sit in Heav'n with thee.

Farewell! friends, whom years of absence
    Had no power to estrange!
Faith in human-kind is strengthened
    By your truth, though all else change.
How I will recall your sayings,
    In my lonely, coming years!—
Precious beacon-lights to cheer me
    O'er my stormy sea of tears!

Farewell! dear old native village!
    What sweet stories are entwined
With each rock, and hill, and islet!
    Must I leave them all behind,
As I onward press to labor—
    Toil and grasp for ends sublime!—
No! mirage-like, I shall view them,
    On the gath'ring mists of time!

This may be a childish worship,
　　But, in almost every mind,
There's a "Holiest of Holies,"
　　Where some idol is enshrined:
And, when I grow old and weary,
　　And from earth would fain be free,
Pilgrim-like, with rev'rent footstep,
　　Mecca-shrine, I'll turn to thee!

Happy, if my native valley
　　Will but hide me in her breast,
And, where those I love lie mold'ring,
　　Lull me peacefully to rest.
Happy, if some loving footstep
　　Will but seek my pillow, wild;
And the tear of pure affection
　　Fall above this wayward child!

August, 1862.

THE DEATH DREAM.

Through the wide casement, the soft moonlight
   Filled, with its glory, a rude, little room;
Touching a sweet face, thin and white,
   And a watcher, who silently wept out his gloom.

Too fair for earth was the beautiful brow,
   And sinless soul of his heart's young bride,
Yet bright was the vision to him, even now,
   Of long, coming years she should walk by his side.

Waking, the blue eyes sought his face,
   And the bright head pillowed itself on his breast,
With a smile that said 'twas the dearest place
   On earth, for the loving one to rest.

"Darling," she said, "I dreamed, to-night,
   That in glory the beautiful clouds unrolled,
Where the sun went down, in a sea of light,
   And molded their mists into gates of gold.

"Silent and pale, from her heights afar,
  Softly the vesper planet shone;
And I thought, as I gazed, that the evening star
  Was what mortals could see of the 'Great White
    Throne.'

"Then away I soared, until, opening wide,
  Swung the golden gates, and I entered in;
And felt, as I left all my guilt outside,
  The rapture of souls that are free from sin.

"Soft arms were about me, and voices sweet;
  And lips that in childhood my forehead pressed,
Were first, 'mong the angel throng, to greet
  The wanderer home, to her welcome rest.

"Teardrops of gladness a moment flowed—
  Like balm and healing they bathed my eyes;
Then down on the golden pavement glowed,
  In precious gems of a thousand dyes.

"The angels told me the beautiful thrones
  And walls and gates and pillars of Heaven
Were made of the tears of repentant ones,
  Who had sinned and suffered, and been forgiven.

"They had all been gathered to deck the home
  That awaited the tread of their weary feet;
Some were chaplets of beauty, and some
  Were fountains that murmured in music sweet.

"Some wafted up, and, in clouds of gold,
  Over the radiant city shone;
Some were gathered, in splendor untold,
  To soften the glory of God's great throne.

"Some were love-light in angel eyes;
  Some were music on angel tongues;
Some swept, in ecstatic melodies,
  O'er harps, and mingled with angel songs.

"Whatever they were, they had all been kept,
  To gladden the mourners when they should be
    free—
And I wondered, if I had repented and wept
  Still more, if Heav'n *could* have been brighter *to me*.

"And they told me the soul that had shed few tears,
  Of repentance and gratitude dear to God,
Was only a child, and must grow for years,
  Ere it knew half the glory of his abode.

"One moment, in meekness, I bowed my head.
  Mute with wonder and gratitude;
Then up from my soul the wild melody sped,
  And I swept my lute and sang 'God is good.'

"Myriad harps, of a myriad tones,
  Caught the measure, and echoed it 'round;
Myriad voices of angelic ones
  Lovingly dwelt on the rapturous sound.

"In forests of perfume, the laden air
  Swept through the green aisles, with Æolian trills;
While footsteps of angels, in joy, everywhere,
  Whispered anthems of praise o'er the heavenly hills!

"The lilies of Heaven clapped their hands,
  And love looked out from their starry eyes;
While crystal waters, o'er golden sands,
  Sang praise to the holy sacrifice.

"And Jesus was there, the beloved and best
  Of the bright host of Heaven, and oh! it was sweet
To feel His smile on me, and lean on His breast,
  And kiss where the nails pierced His hands and
    His feet.

"'Twas a beautiful dream, I seem dreaming it still;
    'Round me angels are hov'ring—I feel their soft
        breath;
And raptures of Heaven my dull senses fill—
    Ah! dearest one! *this* is *no dreaming*—but *death!*"

One passionate moan—one clinging caress—
    One sudden death-pang, and then Life's brittle band
Was shattered, and out from this world's wilderness,
    Together, they went, to that beautiful land!

EXTRACT FROM AN ESSAY ON "MYSTERY."

The flow'r that, with its smiling eye,
  Looks up to us from earth,
Proclaiming to the passer by
  The pow'r that gave it birth;
In its fair form, and way of life,
  Displays a wondrous plan,
That should rebuke the pride, and strife
  For pow'r, twixt man and man.
Yet all is mystery, we know,
  To solve, in vain we try;
Such things we know *are* so and so,
  But *none* can tell us *why!*

We turn our eyes at night, afar,
  Upon the feeble glow
Of light, that started from a star
  A thousand years ago;
And wonder if, through *all of space,*
  Creative pow'r hath been;

And circling worlds have scattered rays
   That man hath *nev'er seen.*
And then we wonder what *is* light?
   And why it never *dies,*
And if at last eternal night
   Will robe the wasted skies!

Thus on we muse, for this faint spark
   Of God, we call the soul,
Would fain leap from its prison dark,
   And comprehend *the whole.*
As waters, from the mountain, leap
   High from their valley bed,
The human soul its goal *will keep*
   High as the *Fountain-head!*

'Tis hard, with all our pride, to think
   Our wisdom is in vain
To learn a single mystic link,
   Of Nature's wondrous chain.
We only know, rock, stream and sea,
   Bird, beast and flow'r and sod—
All things, that *breathe,* that *live,* or *be,*
   Proclaim "THERE IS A GOD!"

LINES TO A FRIEND.

This life a gleam of Heaven would seem,
   If it had nought of sorrow;
But trouble waits, while joy elates,
   To cloud the coming morrow.

God knoweth best: a sweeter rest
   Shall crown our earthly labor,
For ev'ry tear, if, while we're here,
   We love Him, and our neighbor.

If it were mine to 'round thee twine
   Kind Heaven's choicest blessing,
I'd ask for thee a spirit free
   From all complaint, depressing.

Thy patient mind could ever find
   True cause enough for sorrow,
O'er real woes our sad world knows,
   And never need to borrow.

Wherever crime fills up the time
  Of spirits born immortal,
I'd have thee stand with angel hand,
  And point to Heaven's portal.

Where want and grief are, for relief,
  I'd have thee bend in pity;
Each tear will gem thy diadem,
  Within the Mystic City.

And, living thus, sweet memories
  Shall weave their golden glory;
And round thee shine—a light divine,
  While sunny locks grow hoary.

And when, at last, the day is past,
  And angel ones caress thee—
Full many a heart shall feel the smart,
  And countless tongues shall bless thee.

WHISPERS FROM BEYOND.

Silvery murmurs on every side,
   Whispering through the gathering gloom,
Like angel voices, at eventide,
       Lovingly come.

Voices like those of the dear, dead past,
   Sweeter and nearer are softly heard,
'Till I hush, and list! and my heart beats fast!
     Oh! for *one word!*

Vain! 'tis the echo of other things—
   The silvery touch of their airy tread
Or the whispering whirr of their brooding wings,
     Over my head.

WHY FULL OF CARE?

Oh! what is there to make us sad?
 The world is bright and fair;
And everything is gay and glad—
 Why are *we* filled with care?
The little brook, the lowly flow'rs,
 The birds among the trees,
Smile, dream and sing away the hours,
 As careless as the breeze!

There's not a spot, where'er I've strayed,
 Where *all* was sad and drear;
Where not one gleam of gladness played,
 The darkest scenes to cheer;
And, if we cherish, in the heart,
 The sunshine God has giv'n,
We'll save from life full many a smart,
 And make earth almost Heav'n!

A DREAM.

Wierd and strange the scene that bound me;
   Fitfully the quiv'ring gleam
Of the lightning shot around me,
   As I saw it in my dream.
Wildly, frightfully it glinted
   Through the blackness of the night,
And the marble tombstones tinted,
   With its cold, unearthly light.

As I wandered, drenched and weary,
   Through the city of the dead;
With no friendly voice to cheer me,
   And nowhere to lay my head;
Hard and bitter were the feelings
   That arose within my breast,
Till I wooed the very lightning
   Down, to give my spirit rest.

As, with eye and hand uplifted
  To the reckless blaze above,
Hoarsely shrieked I that, in pity,
  'Twould perform that deed of love;
Suddenly I heard a footstep—
  O'er me crept an icy breath—
I remembered I was walking
  In the very home of Death.

Nearer—nearer drew that footstep—
  Low as heart-throb was its fall,
Yet, though raged and roared the tempest,
  Strangely was it heard o'er all.
Closer crept the icy breathing,
  Till each swelling vein was still,
Every weary limb was palsied,
  And my very heart grew chill.

Then a voice, weighed low with anguish,
  Spoke these chiding words to me:
"Thoughtless mortal! art thou tired
  Of earth-life, and wouldst be free?

Woulst thou leave this world of action,
   Ere thy life-task be half done?
Rouse thee to the work that waits thee!
   Ask no crown till it is *won!*"

Then my heart resumed its throbbing—
   Trembling life came back again;
And I saw one near me walking,
- Burdened low with sheaves of grain.
Thin and white his damp locks floated
   On the howling, angry blast;
Dark his sable mantle fluttered
   'Round about him, as he passed.

"Whither walkest thou, oh stranger?"
   Said I to the drooping form,
"Cruel night-winds moan about thee—
   There's no pity in the storm.
Why, for these, leave friends and hearthstone,
   Or hast thou no dwelling place?"
Then a strange, unearthly gleaming
   Overspread his withered face—

Issued from his sombre raiment,
   Till I trembled at the sight—
Till the earth and air was teeming
   With that cold, blue, ghastly light.
"Mortal! dost thou call me stranger?—
   There's no home I enter not—
Cross, unbidden, every threshold,
   Never there to be forgot.

"Whither walk? go ask the tempest,
   Rushing madly to and fro,
All *its* restless, trackless journeys—
   Even *then* ye may not know.
Floating on the breath of morning—
   Resting not at sultry noon,
Wand'ring through the mellow twilight—
   Meeting every one too soon;—

"Through the storm or hush of midnight—
   Onward—stern—unwearied still;—
And the flash in yonder heaven
   Is but vassal to my will.

War and pestilence and famine—
  All these hasten at my word."
Then he leaned him, as one weary,
  On a gleaming, naked sword.

"Men have called me King of Terrors—
  Tried to shun my dreaded way,
But in vain, for all are mortal,
  All must own my awful sway.
Messengers of mine are waiting,
  Wand'ring ever to and fro,—
Some are lurking in the shadows,
  'Neath the laughing waters flow.

"Sting of scorpion, breath of nightshade,
  Wild tornado's blasting sweep—
Trackless oceans' angry billows
  Never weary, never sleep.
Should the weal of future ages
  Ask a mighty city's fall;
Desolating fire and earthquake
  Slumber—*waiting but my call.*

"Scorching wrath of bursting mountains,
　　Molten rock, and lava rain,
For the toil and pride of millions,
　　Leave a silent, vacant plain.
Love and pride are strong—but nothing
　　Can an earthly idol save."
Then he stooped, and laid his burden
　　Down, upon a new-made grave.

And I saw, of what I once thought
　　To be ripe and well filled sheaves,
Some were only worthless branches,
　　Others, little else than leaves.
Myriads of gorgeous flowers,
　　In the beauty of their bloom,
Spread their glowing petals 'mong them,
　　With a witching, strange perfume.

Some, with scarce a leaf unfolded,
　　Had been rudely snatched from earth—
Some, with every petal withered,
　　Bore the glorious fruit of worth.

Then I asked the mighty angel
  "Why should all these flowers die?
Why rob earth of fruits and beauty,
  Leaving such poor stalks as *I?*

"I have wept, and, *longing*, listened
  For the coming of thy feet;
These have shunned thy dreaded visit—
  Life, to them, was bright and sweet."
"Child of earth!" the angel answered,
  "Dost thou think my mission light,
Thus to spread, o'er worth and beauty,
  Poisoned dew and early blight?

"Is it *joy* for me to wander,
  For my awful, primal sin,
'Mong *my children*, shunned and hated,
  Till the last one's gathered in!
Thinkest thou it gives me pleasure,
  Thus to see and aid their fall!
And to hourly feel—my sinning
  Once in Eden, *caused it all!*"

Then a music, low and plaintive,
 As the sobbing autumn breeze,
Strangely heard, among the tossings
 And the moanings of the trees—
Wild, sweet measure, full of sadness,
 Floated solemnly along,
Till all thought and being blended,
 In that sorrow-burdened song.—

"Over the land, and over the sea,
Light and thought less swift than we—
Entering palace, and peasant's cot—
Hated, and never to be forgot—
We choose our victims, and nought can save;—
 Diamonds, and precious gems and gold
Brighten the pageant to the grave,
 But cannot ransom a life once told.—
Hated by him who shared my sin,
 Yet loving him fondly as when of yore
We wandered in Eden's sunny bow'rs,
 Nor dreamed of the destiny hovering o'er!
Oh! the *joy* of existence then!
Days of Eden! come back again!"

Nearer swelled the weeping cadence,
  Then it trembled to a sigh;
And a form, in sombre raiment,
  Passed in mournful silence by.
Every feature, perfect beauty—
  Form and motion, perfect grace;
Heav'n of Love and Hell of anguish
  Met and blended in her face.

Like a cloud she floated onward,
  Murm'ring oft the sad refrain—
"Oh! the bliss that's past forever!
  Eden joys! come back again!"
Half in terror, half in wonder,
  Then I bowed my dizzy head,
While the other caught the measure—
  Wailed it wildly o'er the dead:

"Is there no rest for me?—*evermore*
  Must I wander with grief and tears?
. Is there no quiet, peaceful shore,
  Where I may hide from future years!

Say! may I *never* look upon joy—
   Never listen to mirth and song,
But I must change them to dirges and wo!
   Righteous Father! how long?—how long?"

On he chanted, till the tempest
   Hushed its noisy breath to hear—
Till the moon that lighted Eden
   Smiled again serene and clear—
Till, transported with an anguish
   Keener far than words could say,
Broken grew his dismal measure,
   And the last sound died away.

Then he murmured, "Look up, daughter!"
   Sad, not *fearful*, was his face—
"Look on him who caused all sorrow—
   Father of the human race!
Go! my sword may not yet smite thee,
   Hate thy precious life no more;
Go! be useful, blest and happy
   Till thy active life is o'er.

In my doom the price of sinning
　　Know, and shun such fearful cost;—
In thy life may yet be brightness,
　　And thy future—*what I've lost!*"
As he ceased, an awful darkness
　　Hid him from my mortal sight—
Gloom so palpable—oppressive—
　　I awakened with affright.

Cold the moonbeams fell upon me,
　　In the churchyard all alone;
But the voices I had dreamed of—
　　Sheaves and angels, all were gone.
Giant trees were strewn around me,
　　Lightning-rifted, everywhere;
Dripping locks and drenched garments
　　Told the tempest had been there.
Ghastly white, the marble tombstones
　　'Round me gave the same cold gleam
They had seemed to in my slumber—
　　Yet it must have been a dream!

NIGHT AND MORNING.

ALUMNI POEM, June 16, 1875.

Welcome! bright, restful hour, with love and remem-
  brance teeming;
  Welcome! dear home, whose halls grow dearer with
  gath'ring years;
There's a celestial ray 'mid the glow of our gladness
  streaming—
  Prophecy, dim and fair, of a life that hath done
  with tears!

Each, in this toilsome world, the servant of hard
  Ambition—
  Striving and restless and wild for a share of its
  vain eclat,
Finds, in a grateful word, a more than his hope's
  fruition;
  And sweeter an hour of love than a life of the
  world's huzza!

So, in the rich To Be, that waiteth our fleet life's
    ending,
    Fair though its fragrant groves, and balm though
      its murm'ring air,
Deep though the spirit thrill, with their beauties and
    harmonies blending,
    What were they all to the LOVE that shall clasp us
      forever there !

Some of our precious band have already its radiance
    entered—
    Wooed from a wintry world by a dream of a fairer
      clime:
Wearisome grew the way while their longing hopes
    were centered
    Far in the flow'ry shades of its wonderful summer-
      time.

Dear was thy true life, Laura,* that sped in the
    morning, smiling;
    Heavy the night that fell o'er hearts that had loved
      like ours;

*Miss Laura Rowe, Preceptress, class of '65.

Sweet, o'er its sobbing, rose the music of Faith's
    beguiling,
  That sung of a brighter dawn, in the bliss of im-
    mortal bow'rs!

Marvelous gem art thou, in the crown of our loving
    mother,
  Planet of magic glow in the ether of Memory's
    love!
Ne'er can thy radiance pale in the splendors of
    another,
  For the glory that shines about thee is a ray from
    the world above!

Pure, as the dew, wert thou, that floats to the sky at
    morning;
  Tender and true art thou, safe sheltered from
    earthly strife;
Fitter, for thee, the gems of Heav'n's undreamed
    adorning—
  Best, for thy fine, rare soul, the thrill of a finer life!

Scarce had the pitying sod stole over the grave we
    made thee,
  Scarce had the wildwood flow'rs had time to wither
    and bloom,
Ere, in the forest glade, where we sadly and lovingly
    laid thee,
  Sadly and lovingly laid we our *brother* * in the tomb.

Strange that a soul so rich in itself, and with wealth
    so freighted,
  Drawn from the teeming mines and mints of the
    old and new,
Should, in the glorious day for which we had prayer-
    fully waited,
  Solemnly lift its white wings, and vanish from
    earthly view!

Strange, till we think awhile, and the years that we
    deem so wondrous,
  Sink to but curving swells on the breast of a bound-
    less sea :——

*Professor Wayland Dunn, class of '62.

What are the mines and mints of earth, with their
  treasures pond'rous,
  Viewed from the limitless fields of a blissful
    eternity?

Nor is the labor lost to the soul that departs at
  morning—
  Stronger have grown the pow'rs the infinite depths
    to explore;
Clearer have grown the eyes for the new life's glori-
  ous dawning—
  Keener the sense may thrill to the joys of the
    mystic shore.

Long had he walked on the verge of the valley, and,
  smiling, listened,
  Catching, with ravished ear, the strains from the
    other side:
Narrower fell the stream, till the portals elysian glis-
  tened,
  Fairer than mortal dream, through the vapors
    above the tide.

'Twas "but a step, at most," he said, as he wistfully
    waited—
    Waited the welcome beckon of hands he had loved
        of yore:
Feeling at last the thrill of a traveler weary, belated,
    Ending his desert march, on *his beautiful, native*
        shore!

Peace to the precious dust of our sister and brother
    sleeping!
    Nought can we ask for those who've ascended the
        shining way:
So let our own lives glow with good, that, when done
    with weeping,
    They may, like theirs, be lost in a fuller and fairer
        day!

Not alone for the young is mourning our Alma Mater;
    Not alone to the young be the honors we proudly
        yield:
What of her noble guardians whose triumphs ended
    later—
    Giant, resistless victors, on many a hard fought
        field!

Tenderly cross the hands on the breast that has
    done with sorrow,
  Lovingly close the eyes that forever have done
    with tears
Only *for us* the grief—not a sigh nor a fear we
    borrow,
  For the soul* whose glorious good deeds so
    grandly outweighed his years.

Ever forgetting self, 'twas his to support the falling—
  Fanning to living flame, the hopes that might soon
    depart;
He had a ready ear for the voice of the needy
    calling—
  There was no meed, for him, like the glow of a
    grateful heart!

So, when our Alma Mater languished in early weak-
    ness,
  His was the warm, true heart, that prompted the
    skilful hand;

*Hon. Daniel Dunakin.

His was the loyal soul that ever, in Christian meekness,

Held what he had of wealth as only at God's com-
mand!   .

.

Now, in the beautiful land of the blessed, the gener-
ous giver,

Crowned with eternal peace, whose gladness no
tongue may sing,

Done with the toil and pain and sorrows of earth
forever,

Hath *his reward* at last, from the hand of his
Father King!

Scarce had our sighing hearts accepted the sorrowful
message,

Silently asking who should follow his upward tread,

When, from the thickening clouds of heavy and
direful presage,

Flashed the sad truth to us of another chieftain
dead!

Long shall we miss *thee*, Day,* thou veteran, honored
    and worthy!
  Long shall we miss the skill and force of thy
    guiding hand:
Much do we owe to thee for this monument gleaming
    o'er thee,
  Stately and fair and bright as the best in our sover-
    eign land.

Folded—thy hands, that never yet faltered in right-
    eous doing—
  Silent—thy silver voice, that ever was raised for
    right—
Palsied—thy eager feet, the path of the just pursu-
    ing—
  Vanished—thy noontide glow, in the gloom of
    o'erwhelming night!

Many the faithful ones who have fallen since last we
    parted:
  Many the weary feet that have crossed to the
    shining shore:

*Rev. George T. Day, D.D.

When the far death-knell sounded, bitter the tears
    that started
  Over our girlhood's treasure, our gentle Julia
    Moore.*

Early, alas! she drooped, like some tender and
    tropical flow'r,
  Torn by the piercing blast of a clime too rude and
    chill;
Sweet, that we held her rich, rare bloom one precious
    hour—
  Sweet, we may know in Heaven she is blooming
    for us still!

Calmly she walked among us, pure and serene and
    lowly,
  Holding the words of life with the meekness of a
    child,
Shedding her crescent light, till these dear old haunts
    are holy,
Blessed, for those bright, brief days, with her presence
    undefiled.

*Mrs. Julia Moore Jordan, Preceptress.

Long shall her virtues shine o'er the path she has
    trod before us;
  Ever her voice be missed from the halls we have
    loved so long;
So shall our loving praise, in ever repeating chorus,
  Dearer to her arise, and sweeter than poet's song!

Not alone for the hands that have toiled for our
    loving mother
  Rises the heartfelt tear, or the mourner's voice
    to-day:
Many the names remembered, of sister and of brother,
  Who, like the dew, have vanished, in the morning's
    early ray.

Gone, with the fairy gleam of Life's gay spring about
    them—
  Gone, with their glowing dreams of a long life
    wondrous fair!
Wearily blank grows life, in the homes that are blank
    without them;
  Wearily sighs the soul 'neath the weight of its
    wounding care!

All that they might have been, is not for our mortal
    guessing;
  All that they *were* we honor, and garland with love
    ~~serene~~ *sincere* :
Nor may we Heaven chide for their earthly live's
    suppressing—
  Fitter our grateful praise *for the years He left them
    here!*

Peace to the precious dead, and strength to the
    precious living—
  Strength for the heavier burden, and zeal for the
    fiercer strife!
All that we have of good is only of God's kind
    giving—
  All that we may return is only an earnest life!

Steady the iron heart of Time is forever beating—
  Ages of wondrous deeds are born of these little
    years:
History calmly ebbs and flows with a strange repeat-
    ing,
  Borrowing light and shade from these little smiles
    and tears.

Scatter the flow'rs of Love on the graves of the fair
    dead summers!
  Golden their billows rise through the haze of the
    hallowed past:
Garland the flow'rs of Love on the brows of the
    bright new-comers—
  What they may bring for us, we are glad we may
    not forecast.

It is enough, to-day, to look in the dear old faces—
  List to each well known voice, and grasp the fami-
    liar hand—
Talk of the blest Lang Syne, and dream of the fair
    oases,
  Where we may camp again, on our way through
    the thirsty land!

LITTLE "PET."

The mem'ry, now, seems like a dream,
    And yet I know 'tis true;
A bright, alas! a transient gleam
    I nevermore may view.
'Tis sweet to think about the loved,
    Though they are with the dead;
They never seem indeed removed,
    Their tones are never fled!

This bonny lock hath brushed her brow,
    This ring her finger prest—
I gaze in sadness on them now,
    For she is laid to rest.
These little, withered, wildwood flow'rs
    For me her fingers tied:—
Like her, they bloomed a few short hours,
    Like her, they drooped, and died!

A trifling gift I deemed them then,
  And laid them lightly by;
But now they bring her back again,
  Till moisture dims my eye.
I almost see her sunny face,
  And hear her bounding tread,
And listen to her winning voice—
  I *cannot* think her *dead!*

'Twas very hard to lay her low—
  The sunshine of our home—
The cherished bud—but then we know
  The lost in Heaven will bloom.
I'll meekly try to bear the blow
  My God in love hath given:
He took my treasure home, I know,
  To draw me nearer Heaven!

GOD KNOWETH BEST.

God knoweth best, though years of bitter sorrow
    Weary thy soul, and cloud thy earthly life;
We know there cometh soon a brighter morrow,
    A rest, and gladness after all the strife.

Riches may fail, and all the pow'r they lend thee,
    And proud Ambition die within thy breast;
Then, sweet to know a Father doth befriend thee,
    And tune thy heart to sing God knoweth best.

When dark temptation wearies thee and tries thee,
    Till thou dost almost sink and faint for rest,
Cheer up, and know in love God doth chastise thee,
    Thy victory is strength—He knoweth best.

Dear Father! let what trial *may* come o'er us—
    Still let us lean upon thy loving breast;
Dark though the *past*, the way is *bright before* us,
    While we can meekly say God knoweth best!

TO VIRA C——.

In the beautiful past, there are names that we love,
  Which like stars in the heavens lie aglow;
And their light meets our eye through the haze in the
    sky,
  From the realm of the sweet Long Ago.
Though the storm-cloud arise, and o'erspread all our
    skies,
  Still the magic light flushes the haze;—
Oh! thus, may our love for each other unchanged,
  Light the mem'ry of these happy days!

WORK AS WELL AS PRAY.

Though your heart may never weary,
   Waiting through the lonely night;—
Though your hearth may still be cheery—
   Ne'er have known the wine-cup's blight;
Think of those who daily sorrow
   O'er some darling gone astray;
For the sunshine of *their* morrow,
   Up and *work* as well as *pray!*

Though no wealth you have to offer,
   You can always give good cheer;
Better, far, than burdened coffer,
   Often comes the heartfelt tear.
To the noble cause we cherish,
   You can give your heart and voice;
Holy deeds can never perish—
   Loving words the Heavens rejoice!

TO ———.

When the misty future changes
  These bright days to memories;
And thy fancy fondly ranges
  O'er their quiet happiness;

'Mong the friends that made them cheery,
  Link this humble name of mine;
Hide the faults that make me weary—
  Simply let my *friendship* shine!

There's a home, whose vernal glory
  Haunts me, when I close my eyes—
Fairer forms than dwell in story—
  Flow'rs that bloom not 'neath the skies—

Harps that yield their rapturous measure .
  Only to the courts above;
And the joy-awaking treasure,
  Of that beauteous land, is Love.

Oh! when Death, with chilling finger,
  Points us from this world of care,
Let that treasure with us linger—
  Let us love each other there!

POEM, DELIVERED AT THE QUINQUENNIAL RE-UNION

OF THE

ALUMNI OF HILLSDALE COLLEGE,

JUNE 15TH, 1870.

From tumult and toil, and the din of life's battle,
    On furlough we haste, to the home of our love.
The heart of the mother, that waits for our coming,
    Is true as the Heav'n that is smiling above.

Youth leaps in our veins, as we answer her summons,
    Unmindful of years that upon us have rolled:
We say "boys" and "girls" when we talk of each other, .
    We speak from the *soul,* and *that never grows old!*

The June roses blush at the kiss of the sunshine,
    The lily-buds laugh for their love of the lea;
And birds of the woodland, from hilltop and valley,
    Pour out a sweet welcome of caroling glee!

Yet not *all* is gladness, for Sorrow is brooding,

    With shadowy wiñg, o'er the hearts of our band;

For some that we loved, and who once were among us,

    Have gone, at the beckon of God's loving hand.

In youth they were dear, and, as time wore upon us,

    We learned but the better their virtues to prize;

But we'll meet them no more, till we cross the bright
        threshold

    Of that mystical home, where the soul never sighs!

Our strife may be hard, and our skies often lower,

    Till courage and joy spread their wings to depart;

Yet still, like a perfume of magical power,

    Their mem'ry shall linger to gladden each heart.

Though the Father of love give us singing or mourn-
        ing,

    We know that in mercy he opens his hand;

And, kneeling before him, we meekly adore him,

    And pray for a blessing on us, and our Land.

Oh! wonderful land, with her valleys of vineyards,
    Her vast, lowing herds, and her mountains of ore!
No gem is so rare that her brow does not wear it—
    No want of the *world* can endanger her store!

Her girdle of iron links ocean with ocean;
    Her forests, unmeasured, the world might sustain;
Her shipping, uncounted, ploughs wealth from her
        rivers,
    And a common mart makes of the desolate main!

And still there are mountains and valleys and prairies
    . That wake to no sound but the song of the bird:
There are solitudes deep, in whose wildness unbroken,
    The tramp of the white man has never been heard!

Oh! beautiful land! Fairer skies than Italia's
    Hang over thy mountains, and burnish their haze!
No hues of the Orient can mimic their purple,
    Or vie with the gold of their sun-sinking blaze!

And bright, flitting birds, with their plumage of crim-
        son,
    Sip nectar from flow'rets of tropical dye:
Oh! land of my birth, God hath breathed his own
        spirit
    Upon thee, till thou mayst with Paradise vie!

In beauty and strength, through the dusk of the ages,
 Prophetic thy pillars shine forth on my sight;
Thy presence repeating the proverb of sages—
 "Eternal the structure supported by right!"

Yes, glorious land, 'neath the shade of thy banner,
 The poor and oppressed ever find a sweet home;
The golden grain waves in the fields of their tilling,
 And kindly invites all the needy to come.

Thy schoolhouses teem with the sons of all nations,
 Thy colleges claim them with honor and pride;
There's no caste of wealth, and there's no caste of
 color,—
 On the throne of our country they sit side by side!

'Twas not ever thus; we with sadness remember
 When the chains of our bondmen were riveted
 strong;
When a vile Congress blackened our laws, and its
 mem'ry,
 By lending its voice to oppression and wrong.

But the heart of the nation beat true at the center,
  And freemen, united, arose, and withstood
The giants of evil, till hilltop and valley
  Blushed out the foul shame, in a deluge of blood!

Like gems on the breast of the bright sunny south-
    land,
  Green hillocks lie thick, where our heroes repose;
They fell—and forever their names shall awaken
  The homage of friends, and the honor of foes!

One stain still dishonors the flag of our country,
  And may call for blood from the hearts we love
    best:
It makes us the by-word of civilzed nations,
  It blackens the heart of our beautiful West.

Go fill up the coffers that war has just wasted,
  Go fill up the garners, for loved ones at home!
Be statesmen, in earnest—the gall we have tasted
  Is but too prophetic of strife that must come!

But when, with pure heart, woman stands as the helper
  And equal of man,—soon may usher the day—
The demon of crime, that debases and thralls us,
  Must let go the nation and hasten away.

Not quick, as by force, but as vanished the millions
  Of strange, frightful creatures that roamed o'er the
    earth,
And breathed her crude poison, and fed upon mon-
    sters,
  In armies of terror, ere man came to birth.

The vapory vail of creation was rended;
  The *sunlight* crept into their caverns of slime;
The *pure air* appalled and dispersed them, scarce
    leaving
  A trace on the rude, rocky tablet of Time!

So Love shall illume, and the great heart maternal
  Shall beat for her daughters and sons, then as now;
That Love shall be crowned with a vict'ry supernal,
  As crime and intemperance waver and bow!

Oh! give but the power to those who now sorrow
  In vain o'er the frenzy of those they love best—
How soon would be lightened the load of their
    anguish,
  And singing be heard in the happy home nest!

Fear not! ne'er can liberty rob her of home-love
  Or gentleness—You would not fear that the vine,
Transplanted from cellar to garden, and flinging
  Its boughs to the breezes, would e'er be a pine!

The wind and the tempest may visit it harshly;
   Its tendrils may shrink from the midsummer sun;
While broad spread the branches, with strength for
     their burden
   Of fruit, that is yours when the harvest is done!

My Michigan! dearest and best of our number!
   All honor to thee for that triumph of right
Which opened the halls of our pride to thy daughters—
   Let History write it in letters of light!

Thy record is fair as the sky that hangs o'er thee,
   As breath of the prairie thy spirit is free:
To the grand march of progress thy footsteps are
     hast'ning,
   As hasten thy lakes to the surge of the sea.

The beauty of truth through thy vestment is shining,
   Like perfume, thy liberty sweetens the gale;
Nor least of thy gems is our dear Alma Mater—
   Her light be our beacon, and *ne'er may it pale!*

How oft have our voices awakened her echoes,
   In times that grow sacred with gathering years!
The visions of Lang Syne arise, rainbow-tinted,
   To us, as we view them through fast rising tears!

Dear home of my youth! may the fame of thy future
  Be fair as thy past, in its palmiest day;
May concord, and kind emulation uplift thee,
  And golden endowment untrammel thy sway!

The ivy of love be thy bond and thy beauty,
  And brighten its green whene'er clouds dim the sky;
Beneath thee, like granite, may temp'rance and justice
  Thy columns uphold, and thy ruin defy!

Dear brothers and sisters, we part, and the billows
  That part us may never their power withhold;
But ties have been formed, in this circle fraternal,
  More lasting than time, and more precious than
    gold.

The principles dearest to each of our number
  Are links that might well our great Commonwealth
    bind:
Be Justice her shield, and, adown in the future,
  Her arms may encircle and bless *all mankind!*

May her time-tested banner float ever above us—
  All bright be its stripes, and undimmed every star,
While we swear, by the hearts that we love and that
    love us,
  To revere it in peace, and avenge it in war!

THE FORSAKEN HOME.

Sister, I've wandered to the home,
  Where we, in childhood played;
Nor dreamed that, in these few fleet years,
  We could so far have strayed.
The robins chirp among the trees,
  As blithe as when, before,
We clinked our jack-stones on the lawn,
  Before the cottage door.

The walnut tree, down by the spring,
  Where swaying grapevines hung;
And where, with hearts as pure and free
  As the waters there, we swung,
Is cut away, but one is left,
  Where, often, you and I
Gathered the falling nuts, beneath
  The hazy, autumn sky.

You know we wandered in the woods,
  One Indian-summer day,
And dug up all the wild-flow'r roots,
  We found along the way;

And planted in the little spot
   We called our garden then;—
I sought, but found them not, the place
   Had grown to grass again.

The dear old home looks desolate,
   And everything around;
And the wind sweeps through the vacant hall,
   With a sad and weary sound.
In empty rooms I hear a tone—
   The voice of an echo sweet,
But vainly look for the dear ones gone,
   And list their coming feet.

'Tis but the house, the dear old house,
   And yet it seems to feel,
Or to *have felt*, the yearning pain,
   That *will* upon *me* steal.
Mournful and dumb, it still remains,
   Pathetic—crumbling—dead—
From which the living, loving band,
   Which was its soul, has fled!

SUSPENSE.

Darling sister, when the twilight
    Like an angel cometh down,
(With the vesper star, that dimly
    Burns above the dusty town)
      How the flooding memories flow
      From the gladsome long ago.

Daytime with its cares and bustle,
    Anxious greed and strife for pelf
Fills and kills the hours till twilight
    Kindly woos our thoughts from self,
      And our weary spirits roam,
      Backward, to our father's home.

How its dear old shadows haunt me,
    When I close my tearful eyes!
How the murmurs of its voices,
    Round my loneliness, arise;
      Till, within its humble door,
      We seem gathered, as of yore.

Precious Mem'ry! ever faithful
  Art thou to thy sacred trust!
Thou hast garnered up my sunlight,
  Though its source hath turned to dust,
    And amid these sadder days,
    I can bask me in its rays.

In the quiet village graveyard,
  We have made *one* mound—no more,
You and I are left, but, sister,
  In our loved home-band were *four*—
    "Where! Oh! where does father lie?"
    Comes no answer to our cry?

In the glowing, sunny southland,
  Where the wild magnolia blooms,
Hovering its pitying fragrance
  O'er unnamed, unnumbered tombs—
    'Mong the faithful and the brave,
    Did some comrade make his grave.

Or upon the scorching marshland
  Of a dreary prison pen, .
Did he starve and pine and perish,
  With our hosts of noble men?
    "Missing!" Oh the pang intense
    Of this dreary, long suspense!

Helpless, crazed, forsaken, sightless,
　Does he *beg* from door to door,
Dreaming vaguely of the loved ones,
　Who may never see him more—
　　Gazing far through ceaseless tears
　　On the bliss of other years?

In his *dreams*, do mem'ries hover,
　Clear as noonday's cloudless skies
Till amid the day's drear turmoil
　Only *glimpses* may arise,
　　That shine out upon the strife
　　Like a gleam of some old life?

No! such portion were *too bitter*—
　Let us not believe it so—
Rather let us think he perished
　With his hand against the foe,
　　And the Southern soil was red
　　With *his* blood where *heroes* bled.

Father! when thou wert among us,
　We unfaithful oft have proved
Oft unheeding—oft in anger—
　Grieved thee, while we *deeply loved*—
　　Now, the *hardest* of our woe
　　Is—*we cannot tell thee so.*

On thy patient loving bosom
  Oh! to weep our grief away!
Oh! by years of thoughtful kindness
  Some of our *great debt* to pay!
    How our weary hearts have bled
    For *the wrongs we've done the dead!*

Hand in hand, among the blessed,—
  Ye are safe and joyous now
Angel father—angel mother—
  Crowns of good deeds on each brow.
    May *our* brows such garlands wear
    When at last we meet you there!

Sister! Earth is full of sorrow,
  But it bringeth bliss as deep,
We can joy in *kindness* only
  After we have learned to *weep.*
    Both our hearts have *kinder* grown
    For the *sorrows* they have known.

TO THE HON. MR. H——, AND LADY.

COMPLIMENTS AND REGRETS OF MR. AND MRS. J— C— P——,

FOR THURSDAY EVENING, SEPT. 4TH.

Regret is deep and vast and vain—
    We cannot be among you,
To help the noise, or swell the train
    That bother, bless and throng you.

But may a Presence more than ours,
    Be with your nuptial meeting;
Nor on the new home cease its show'rs,
    While Time is onward fleeting.

'Tis strange, alas! that 'tis so strange—
    The dear ones we have sainted,
To merely earthly beings change,
    When once we're well acquainted.

Life often leads us far apart,
  Through dreary, wounding places,
Ere love has learned his holiest art,
  Or sweetest of embraces.

Forbearance is a wholesome cup,
  And, by it, lives are blended;
Well—there! the baby's waking up!—
  But then my sermon's ended.

TO A FLOWER.

Beautiful, lonely, snow-white flow'r!
    Thou hast brightened my dusky room,
Many a sad and toilsome hour,
    With thy innocence and perfume.
No one is here to scorn the tears
    That *will* rise at the sight of thee—
None to roll back the sober years,
    And talk of the good old times with me.

Thou art my only treasure now—
    Once I'd a garden, all my own,
Loved and cherished, but not as thou—
    Dearer treasures were not yet flown.
And, as their memories come and go,
    And I gaze, through my tears, on thee,
These days are hidden, and I grow,
    Childish, but not in gayety.

Starry-eyed flowers bloomed for me then,
    Petals as purely white as thine—
May be their spirits rose again,
    Watchful o'er this dark path of mine.
I used to think they knew me, then,
    Used to woo them to speak to me—
Tell them my plans, and think they smiled,
    Sharing in all my guileless glee.

Time has been busy, since then, I trow,
    Filling my heart with anguish and sin;
I have wandered, unguided, till now,
    Little is worthy of love, within.
On! to the future, Ambition wooes,
    And I helplessly follow on:
Fame for Love is a poor excuse,
    But soul must have *something* to feed upon:

Just as my little drooping flow'r,
    Torn from its mother, and the light,
Feeds upon *water*, for an hour—
    Something to put off utter night!

APRIL 30TH.

Now thou art dying, my little pet—
   What! art thou tired of life so soon?
Live on! nor leave me in darkness yet—
   Live! till thy morning has warmed to noon!

Other flowers may bloom and fall,
   Flinging a gladness o'er my heart;
But thou weavest, beyond them all,
   Mem'ries that·never can depart.
And I'll cherish thy petals brown,
   Sacredly, all life's little hour—
Precious dust of my silent one,—
   Once my beautiful, snow-white flow'r!

EIGHTEEN.

Another changeful year has fled,
　　Though scarce it seemed begun—
A year of strife, with sorrow rife,
　　And vict'ries sin hath won.
When thoughtlessly I hailed its birth,
　　With wild festivity,
I little dreamed the agony
　　The "New Year" held for me.

My heart was young and light and free,
　　Few sorrows yet had come,
To chill my careless, childish glee,
　　And blight my spirits' bloom.
Would that I might be joyous now,
　　E'en for one hour, and feel
This haunting shadow off my brow—
　　This weight of Sorrow's seal.

Would that these weary feet might stray,
   Where once, in happier days,
I knelt beside my mother's knee,
   And learned my Maker's praise.
Oh! happy hours! Oh! vanished hours!
   I weep, but *must not* weep—
My buried treasures—hidden flowers—
   For me the *angels* keep!

That precious form is laid to rest,
   But Mem'ry lingers still,
And loves to linger o'er the page
   My mother's actions fill.
Oh! is there aught that shields the soul
   Whene'er temptation's flame,
In scorching surges, o'er it sweeps,
   It is that sacred name!

She went—the tend'rest tie is riven—
   And she is happier there;
I would not call her down from Heaven
   To breathe earth's blighting air.

Yet, could she know, by angel art,
　　The wand'rings of her child—
Could look into this wayward heart,
　　And see its passions wild:

If tears could enter Heaven, a tear
　　Would gem that angel's eye,
And she would fly to earth, and bear
　　My spirit to the sky.
And now another year has come—
　　A curious blank to me
Is its strange freight of light and gloom—
　　What will this new year be?

BY-AND-BY.

On the beautiful banks of the river of Peace,
   There are flow'rs that can never decay;
There the brightness of fond eyes shall nevermore
      cease,
   Or death bear our loved ones away.

No sickness or sorrow, no passion or pride,
   Have a place in that blissful abode;
In gladness immortal, love, side by side,
   We shall dwell in the city of God.

Oh! sweet, on the banks of that mystical stream,
   To drink in the music of Heaven;
And remember this life as a far away dream,
   Whose follies and sins are forgiven!

TO J—.

Thou art a diamond!—In that night,
   When Sorrow held her gloomy sway,
I caught the glimmer of thy light,
   And hoped, while waiting for the day!

ALL ABOUT BLACKBIRDS.

FOR THE TWO LITTLE BOYS.

Welcome! noisy, merry blackbirds!
  Once again ye herald spring,
With your gleeful, roguish chatter—
  What a world of joy ye bring!
Dreams of violets and snowdrops,
  Springing grass, and budding trees
Melt away, in sweet fulfilling,
  'Neath the music-laden breeze!

Little shining, scolding blackbirds!
  Think not ye are strange to me;
Many a time I've wept to save you,
  In a childhood agony!
I have argued that my blackbirds
  Had a *right* to papa's wheat:—
"Sure—'twas cruel to deprive them
  Of what little *they* could *eat.*"

And I volunteered, my birdies
　　All my wondrous help to give—
Scaring you from all the wheatfields—
　　If he'd only let you live.
So, the long, bright days, I wandered,
　　Up and down the mellow field,
Flags and rags; a fright to blackbirds,
　　Yet my birdies' only shield.

Then chirp on your merry music!
　　For, though now a woman grown,
Nought shall harm the thieving rascals
　　That I plead for once alone.
And remember, please, while peering
　　Down so queerly from that tree,
That your *grandpas* would have perished,
　　If it had not been for me!

"ONE MAN MISSING."

Do ye tell me "he is dead—"
   That the glowing hopes I've cherished,
Since our nuptial vows were said,
   In the battle gloom have perished!
Then farewell, for aye, to mirth—
   Let my bruised heart *break* with sorrow—
Lay me in the still, cold earth—
   There's no meeting on the morrow!

I can see him on the field—
   None to soothe, and none to save him—
Dying, where he would not yield,
   From the wounds a traitor gave him.
I can feel his thirst and pain,
   See him pale and sink and languish,—
See him prone among the slain,
   In his depth of dying anguish.

'Then away! your songs of glee—
　Dancing feet, and merry seeming!
What is all your joy to me,
　With this woe upon me streaming?
Let my wounded spirit weep,
　Till its throes are numb with sorrow!
In the dark earth hide me deep!—
　There's no meeting on the morrow!

MRS. SHODDY.

Poor Mrs. Shoddy! what ado
   You make, with lace and feathers;
To one so lately fledged as you,
   They seem the worst of tethers.

You try to speak—your voice is loud—
   You straightway have to calm it:
Your smothered Self resists its shroud,
   Nor Egypt could embalm it.

The ruche around your chubby chin,
   Would grace, as well, your poodle;
And diamond rings, and diamond pin,
   But plainer speak the noodle.

You've stepped upon your costly gown,
   And, lack-a-day! have torn it;
And loudly tell us, with a frown,
   It was the first you'd worn it.

You roll your eyes, and spread your train,
    And sweep us like a duster;
Till we are forced to smile again,
    In wonder at your bluster.

That little woman, plain and fair,
    In dress that's almost fady,
Wears not a jewel, here or there,
    And yet we call her *lady*.

Not days of wealth, but years of worth
    Must bring the place you covet:
While you're a worm, remain on earth,
    Nor seek to soar above it.

The brightest names, the richest lives,
    The bluest blood in story,
Are those of quiet, plain housewives,
    Whose dress was not their glory.

With them the pudding-stick and broom
    Were friendly, useful neighbors;
And, at the spinning-wheel and loom,
    They gloried in their labors.

That day of toil, of course, is passed,
 But still their daughters linger,
With modest eye, and thoughtful cast,
 And ever helpful finger.

You know them by their gentle "No,"
 Or gentler acquiescence;
They have a way of *list'ning* so,
 They shame your noisy presence.

If plainly clad, to garments' hem,
 They do not seem to know it:
If crowned with diamond diadem,
 They do not try to show it.

Then, Mrs. Shoddy, cease to strive,
 Nor chase us with your basket;
For common folks delight to give
 To those who do not ask it.

Nor hope to gain the boon you ask,
 Before your worth deserves it:
Still *then* remains the weightier task,
 For *worth alone preserves it.*

LINES ON THE DEATH OF A LITTLE CHILD.

Oh! vain is the fond heart's weeping,
   And the gloom of these heavy hours;
For our darling boy lies sleeping,
   With the rest of the summer flow'rs!

No sin or suff'ring or sorrow
   May ever his dear eyes dim;
No grief, that may visit *our* morrow,
   Can take one rapture from *him!*

So Faith, 'mid our sorrow, sits singing,
   And will sing, through the dark days to come;
Till we hear his sweet voice, again, ringing
   Our welcome to God's sweet home!

A SIGH.

Strange, how fitful, frail and fleeting,
  All our earthly pleasures seem!—
Ere we know them, swift retreating,
  Like the mem'ry of a dream.
Brightest eyes will lose their brightness,
  Sunny locks be turned to grey—
Bounding footsteps lose their lightness—
  All that's earthly, change, decay.

Life has very much of sadness,
  Very much of grief and pain—
Much to chill and check our gladness,
  Sicken heart, and weary brain.
Fondest hearts will grow forgetful,
  Forms we love will turn to dust,—
Friendship's chain be rudely broken,
  Or, forgotten, dim with rust.

Sad indeed would be our portion,
  Were our hopes all centered here,—
Souls, expanding and immortal,
  Chained within this narrow sphere;
But a brighter, clearer prospect,
  To our toiling race is giv'n,—
Lasting bliss, and purer pleasures,
  Peace and truth are found in Heav'n.

POEM DELIVERED AT THE DEDICATION OF THE SOCIETY HALL

OF THE

ECLECTICS AND ATHENIADES,

ALBION COLLEGE, APRIL 1869.

We come! we come! from the roar of the billows,

    That beat the gray rocks of the New England shore;

We come from the West, from the wide stretching
      prairies,

    Where wild deer and buffalo graze at our door:

From the far distant hills, where the rocks are of silver,

    From streamlets where diamonds and gold lie
      aglow;

From the northland of song, from the haunt of the
      red man,

    Where the silvery birch, and the cottonwood grow.

We come from the shore where the orange tree blos-
      soms,

    And the coral reef lurks in the smile of the sea;

We come from the fields where we offered our
      'brothers,

    That this might, in truth, be "the land of the *free!*"

We come in our youth, with a life-time before us,
　　With garlands and music, and festival glee:
No repining of ours shall invade the glad chorus,
　　But the night shall be bright as the surf of the sea.

And we, in mid-age, from the cares that have bound
　　　　us,
　　Come home, with glad hearts, for an hour, to be
　　　　free,
And echo the song that is ringing around us—
　　"The night shall be bright as the surf of the sea."

We forget, for the while, all the wrecks that are
　　　　scattered
　　In the caves of the sea, 'neath the sun-tinted foam;
The gay dreams dispelled, and the darling hopes
　　　　shattered,
　　Forget, while we answer the sweet "Welcome
　　　　home!"

And we, at the gloaming, return from our roaming,
　　With hearts more content than when life was half
　　　　o'er;
A sweeter reposing steals on, at life's closing,
　　And we learn to live over the bright days of yore.

Oh! the beautiful past, with its archway of sunshine,
   That flushes the haze with a halo of gold!
Oh! magical haven of dreams that are vanished!
   Sweet Eden of thought for a life almost told!

The joy of to-night is a gleam from its portals;
   This music, a chime from that Aiden of earth!
So we, at the gloaming come back from our roaming,
   To mingle our song with the holiday mirth.

Yet not as of old do we gather our numbers,
   Where daily we climed up the fabulous "hill—"
A temple more meet we turn gladly to greet,
   And the dear circle here makes it *home for us still.*

What gems can we bring to most fitly adorn it?
   Shall diamonds and rubies flash envious light?
Shall drapings of damask and gold half enclose it,
   And lend to the day the soft splendors of night!

Yes, diamonds of thought, with their keen, cutting
     polish,
   To penetrate darkness, and error invade;
And rubies of kindness, to soften and brighten
   The channel the merciless diamond has made.

But drape it with evergreen, twine it with flowers,
  Let nought the free life-breath of knowledge arrest;
Then muses shall gather their bright numbers hither,
  Our words to inspire at the gentlest behest.

Let Science and History guard at its portals;
  Let Poesy strew it with garlands of song;
Let Art carve its cornices, people its niches,
  And whisper sweet music its pillars among.

Let Truth sit enthroned, in her meekness and white-
    ness,
  Where weekly we gather, her stores to unfold,
Then charming our temple, and peerless her treasures,
  More brilliant and lasting and precious than gold.

But whence the foundation for temple so wondrous?
  Shall columns so fair plant their feet in the earth?
Shall Time touch their beauty, and mar them with
    mildew,
  And sink in decay all their splendor and worth?

From the hum of the past come the voices of millions,
  Who built on the earth, but whose building was vain;
Their marble is dust, and their laurels have perished,
  And nothing is left but this hopeless refrain :—

"Ambition" our guide, and earth's honor our goal,
　　We have toiled but in vain through a .wearisome
　　　　strife;
For Fame has forgotten our names to enroll,
　　Though we flattered and wooed her, and gave her
　　　　our life.

We have searched into Nature's mysterious tome,
　　We have drawn the quivering flash from heaven,
And laughed at its tame and obedient path,
　　O'er the towers and forests it erst had riven!

We have grasped the storm, in its howl and shriek,
　　Have measured its power, and scorned its might;
We have tortured the rocks till we made them speak,
　　And tell us the story of Time's whole flight!

The wondrous world that we could not win,
　　We have weighed, and measured the land and sea;
And challenged the very stars to hide
　　Their mazy paths in immensity!

Like a seer of old, to the list'ning land,
　　We have told the days of a darkened sun,
Or a comet's course, and, as though in our hand
　　The universe circled, the work was done!

We have traced with chisel the clust'ring vine,
 The column of beauty to crown and enwreathe,
And statues, so teeming with mimic life,
 We almost listened to hear them breathe!

We have caught the pencil, and prisoned the blaze
 Of clouds that pillowed the sinking sun;
And mellowed his rays in the silvery haze
 That lingers around when the day is done!

We have swept the lyre till a wondering world
 Stood still, entranced by the strain sublime;
We thought it would echo till earth was no more,
 And live to murmur the dirge of Time!

Oh, vain, all the hoping and toil of a life!
 The strings are all silent, the statue o'erthrown,
The column and capital mingle their dust,
 And the sun-tinted canvas lies mold'ring unknown!

The knowledge we gained intermingles with time;
 And temples like ours lift their arches of pride;
But their builder shall sleep in oblivious deep,
 If self is his god, and ambition his guide!"

Oh, Charity! beautiful, gentle and holy!

    Accept the poor homage we yield at thy feet,

Come, dwell in our circle, unite and inspire us,

    To make for each pillar a pedestal meet!

Oh, Liberty! sacred, benign and majestic!

    Of all men alike the beloved and desired,—

Come breathe in our counsels, and make this a temple

    Where statesman are nourished, and patriots in-
        spired!

Oh! Author of Liberty! Father of Charity!

    Guardian of all that is sacred and dear!

Still low are our aims, and in vain all our labors,

    If thou smile not upon us, or meet with us here!

Where self sits enthroned, may she sink in confusion,

    And low at thy feet bow her penitent knee;

Oh! then may we bend, a fraternity holy,

    In labor for man, and in homage to Thee!

Inspire thou our hearts, and when ages have perished

    Our names shall, unsought, immortality find:

More lasting than laurels of Fame's partial weaving,

    Our *deeds* shall live on, in the *love of mankind!*

THE SOUL CAN NE'ER GROW OLD.

I see the threads of silver gleam,
 Above my forehead, now,
And count the lines, as in a dream,
 That sink upon my brow.

I know, a few short years ago,
 These locks were sunny gold;
This forehead too was smooth, I trow,
 Yet I'm not growing old!

Not growing old—ah no! my heart
 Is in its spring-time yet:
It will *not* let its bloom depart;
 It *will* its years forget.

Why will ye check your guileless mirth,
 When my bent form appears—
Would *ye keep* all the joy of earth,
 And give *me* naught but tears.

I hear you sweetly warble out
   Your dear familiar chime;
And I would fain repeat the shout,
   As in the olden time.

Ye know not what ye speak, who say
   Years wrap the heart in gloom:
Our lives, like any other day,
   Grow brighter towards the tomb.

And Time has flung across my sky
   His wealth of vap'rous gold,
To gladden hopes that cannot die—
   I am not growing old.

Come hither, children! How I prize
   The flick'ring power still
To look into your gleeful eyes,
   And hear your laughter trill!

Ye 'mind me of another band,
   That blessed another hearth:
Alas! as pictures on the sand,
   They vanished from the earth!

These withered lips drank in their love;
　　It made my sunshine then:
This heart grew strong to work, and strove
　　To make them noble men.

They blessed my patient, loving care,
　　But, one by one, they fled:
With them there is no need of prayer,—
　　I do not call them dead.

And soon, I, too, shall yield my breath,
　　And earth my form enfold:
The ripe'ning soul will drop its sheath,
　　But 'tis not growing old.

Then children gather, round my knee
　　Your heads of sunny gold:
Your mirth is music still to me:—
　　The *soul* can *ne'er* grow old!

AT LAST.

Anna, musing at the gateway,
   Leaned her head upon her hand;—
Watched the golden, sunset glory
   Turn the earth to fairy land;—
Watched the dying sunlight glisten
   On her little wedding band.

Homeward marching, worn and dusty,
   Came a weary, soldier-throng:
Soiled and tattered were their garments,
   Fitful were their bursts of song:
Some were very faint and feeble,
   And with anguish crept along.

Anna, weeping, at the gateway.
   Thought how Herbert's name she read,
Years ago, among the missing,
   And she knew he must be dead;
So, while they were marching past her,
   Anna, weeping, bowed her head.

One there was, the last and faintest,
  Fell, upon the dusty way;
No one heeded him save Anna,
  But she sprang to where he lay—
Gently bathed the blanching forehead—
  Wooed the flut'ring soul to stay.

Slow he turned his eyes upon her—
  What a quenchless love-light shone,
In the dying gaze he gave her!—
  Faithful Herbert's march was done!
"You will come to me, my darling'—"
  Low he whispered and was gone.

Anna, musing at the gateway,
  Gazing far through sunset gold,
Weeps no more in doubt, though watching
  Till the sky is gray and cold—
Murmurs "You will meet me darling,
  When the pearly gates unfold!"

NEVER MIND!

Fond Mem'ry, in her kindness,

Will smile upon our blindness,

And wrap these little sorrows in her robe
of misty gold;

And we'll delight to linger,

And point a wrinkled finger

Back to these days, and call them "*The
blessed time of old.*"

CONCERNING A LAWYER'S HANDWRITING.

One night, when my poor, patient Pegasus drooped,
  'Neath his side saddle load, and fell dozing,
My brain, with a protest, to common things stooped,
  And my unwilling pen fell to prosing.

I answered some letters—among them was yours,
  My J—, full of "Dears," "Doves" and "Darlings;"
And, like a huge, cat-worried tangle of silk,
  It held some miraculous snarlings.

The wrinkles I gathered that terrible night
  The day of Doom never will frighten
Quite off from my forehead; but, after it all,
  I had myself *still to enlighten.*

Your g's stood agape, and your l's shook their fists,
  And seemed very wrathy about it;
And one horrid "z," stuck in spatters and mists,
  Seemed rising to smite him who wrote it.

It was just about then that I let the world slide,
    And away to the land of nod drifted,
And dreamed, among many strange matters beside,
    That the latch of my sanctum was lifted;

And in stepped an old man, greyheaded and worn,
    And he walked with a twitch, and a worry,
Which said, very plainly, 'twas business he meant,
    And he'd like to be off in a hurry.

He'd a basket on one arm, a cane in his hand,
    And his beard was full, flowing and hoary;
And he trembled and twitched, but continued to stand,
    While he told me his singular story;—

From the city where all of earth's printing was done,
    The type and the presses had vanished!
The Devil had probably wanted some fun,
    And the hopes of a year or two banished.

For an accident happened, as queer as the one
    Which bothered the masons at Babel;
And, to think how "that old-fashioned printing" was
      done,
    Not a man in the world was yet able.

The making of *paper* was, too, a "lost art"—
  And of *ink*—but he told me, enraptured, .
That the *old stock* would sparingly hold out a *year*,
  When they hoped the said arts would be captured.

They once thought they had them, and made a fair
    start,
  But they cut most incredible capers;
So the chemists were taking the old sort apart,
  And reporting their luck in the papers.

Meanwhile, they were doing as well as they could,
  By gathering old, useless pages,
And cutting the letters apart, and, *on wood*,
  Re-*pasting* the wisdom of sages.

The boards were, of course, of convenient size—
  (Wide awake, it looks rather appalling,
But it seemed quite a natural thing in my sleep,)
  Then he told me his object in calling.

It was for old manuscript, letters or books,
  Or anything written or printed;
He'd pay a round sum for a bushel or so—
  A fortune in fact—so he hinted.

I thought of the poverty barring our way
    To the halter—or altar, you call it—
And of many sad things, till I could'nt say Nay,
    To the plea of my poor, shrunken wallet.

I ran, and brought forward a *bushel*, or more,
    Of *your letters*, I blush to confess it;
But "if 'murder' is in them, it never 'will out,' "
    I thought, "for no mortal could guess it."

He took them, and solemnly turned them about,
    Top side up or down—'twas no matter;
He looked *through* his spectacles, *'neath* them, *above*—
    While my heart went, of course, pit a patter.

He answered at last, and the answer he made
    Was intended, no doubt, to be civil:—
"Well—yes * * * * There's a 'd' or two here, that I think
    I *could use* to commence the word 'Devil'!"

A GLIMPSE OF DOOM.

Down through the glowing West, the sinking sun
   Swept on, with flaming banners all unfurled:
Though glories ever crowned the course he'd run,
   The grandest lingered 'round the dark'ning world.

The distant hum of children's voices fell
   Upon the ear, and note of Whip-poor-will
Its music blended with the tinkling bell
   Of sheep that grazed upon the burnished hill.

Deep in the cooling stream, the toil of day
   All past, unyoked, the thirsty cattle stood:
The whistling farmer trode his homeward way,
   With hardened hand, but honest heart and good.

The gaudy butterfly, with wearied wing,
   Hid from the dew beneath some nodding rose,
And earth had all her share of everything
   That helps the nameless charm of daylight's close.

I saw and heard all, yet exulted not,
  As, with rebellious heart, and footstep slow,
Unthinkingly, I sought the quiet spot,
  Where oft I'd watched the summer sunset glow.

For earth-born passions, hourly through my life,
  Had swayed my struggling spirit by their might;
And I had vainly promised that the strife
  Should end, next hour, in vict'ry of the right.

And once in rashness had I dared to *swear*
  To keep this promise, faithfully and well;
And, in the depth of soul accusing there,
  Had called on Heaven to *curse* me *if I fell!*

I fell! and aught that human heart could know,
  Of self-accusing anguish, scorched my soul;
A sullen ocean of consuming wo,
  Whose billows nevermore could cease to roll.

What recked I that the birds and waters sang,
  And childish laugh my would-be deaf ear cross'd?
Each voice more awful than a demon's rang—
  Were *they* not *pure!* and *I forever lost!*

Long did I gaze into the glowing sky,
 Whose burning depths seemed flaming wrath at me;
And longed yet feared to pray that I might die,
 For what *was* death, to one *accursed, liké me!*

And slowly still the darkness gathered 'round,
 Till sight of spire and cot and wood were gone,—
Till lengthened shadows wrapped the dewy ground,
 And still the angry heavens kept flaming on!

When oh! what awful peal rent earth and sky!
 What burning, vap'ry billows filled the air!
How rose the vales in dizzy cliffs on high!
 What wails of woe! what howlings of despair!

The trembling mountains bowed them in the dust;
 The frightened ocean backward swiftly sped;
And tortured earth upheaved her solid crust,
 Unpeopling all the cities of the dead!

And forth they came, a pale and silent band,
 Till Heav'n aroused the slumb'ring spirits' glow,
And called the faithful to the blest "right hand,"
 And left the shrieking guilty to their woe!

Yet all unnoticed and unharmed *I* stood,

    While swaying millions, parting, swept along:—

The *only one*, of all the multitude,

    Who seemed to have no place in *either* throng.

Spellbound and mute, I watched them as they passed,

    Each brow prophetic of its destiny,

Until the restless clouds enwrapped the *last*—

    Then shrieked—"Oh God! hast thou *forgotten me?*

Is *this* my "curse"?   High rose the trembling plain,

    On which I stood, to mountain crest, that brake,

With solid base, a moaning, crimson main,

    Of molten rock—'twas all Jehovah spake!

And sullen clouds rose from the flaming wave;

    And time wore strangely on—no day—no night—

No light save that the glowing ocean gave,

    For darkened heavens refused to mark its flight.

I listened to the melodies afar

    Of chanting spirits, speeding on their way,

To drink the glories of some unseen star—

    Each soul a heav'n—God's love its perfect day.

And cries of anguish and despair arose
    Unceasingly from Sorrow's dark abode;
And I would fain have plunged me in its woes,
    Could I have fled from thoughts of peace and God.

I thought of childhood's joy, and guileless glee,
    My peaceful home, and mother's lullaby,
And little prayers she taught me at her knee,
    That I might nobly live, and gladly die.

And thus I lived and thought, a conscious thing,
    While sunless ages dragged, unnumbered, by;
No pain from heat or cold or hungering—
    All else forgotten in the wish *to die!*

And, as those ages passed, the seething main
    Gave up its furnace heat, and ceased its flow;
And, o'er the arid, adamantine plain,
    Clouds rested from their wand'rings to and fro.

And cooling showers fell upon the earth,
    Till oceans, in their majesty and might,
Seemed fraught with knowledge, and to mourn the
      dearth
    Of their own waters, and their dusky light.

And still I lived, and knew that ages rolled,
  For fertile valleys filled the ocean's bed,
And forests girt the mountains, as of old,
  And hum of insect broke the silence dread.

And paler grew the heavy mist, that hung,
  In dismal winding sheets of dusky gray;
Till clouds of ancient, snowy splendor swung,
  And earth exulted in a sunlit day.

Oh joy! Oh matchless joy! with starving soul,
  To feast upon the glories pictured there!
Oh agony! to know each burst of hope
  But plunged me deeper in my mad despair!

The laughing water leaped with limpid bound,
  And fragrance born of Heaven filled the breeze;
And flow'rs of matchless beauty wrapped the ground,
  While holy music echoed 'mong the trees.

And creatures came, of wond'rous, glorious mold
  In whom a spark of God's own spirit dwelt,
With symmetry of form and soul untold,
  Whose joy was full, when at his feet they knelt.

No base desires confined them to the dust;
   There was no prayer and toil for "daily bread"—
No hunger, and, in actions good and just,
   Life sped, and no one sorrowed for the dead.

There *was* no death, but one immortal *youth*,
   For those to whom was giv'n the chastened sod;
And an eternal progress unto truth—
   A nearer likeness to their father—God.

And o'er the land or gushing waves they strayed,
   In raiment spotless as the seraphs wear,
Or in the deep sea's pearly chambers played,
   Or swept in brightness through the upper air.

Oh! awful destiny! that I must see
   And feel and know the heav'n on every side,
And yet endure through all eternity
   "Oh Righteous One! Too GREAT my curse!" I
     cried.

"I never dreamed that Heav'n itself could pour,
   On bold, blasphemous soul, a doom like this!
Ye oceans! rise and flood the peaceful shore!
   Fall on me, mountains! Hide me from such bliss!"

Mute—mute—the solemn hills, in grand repose,
   Saw not, heard not my awful agony;
While joyously the crystal waves arose,
   And mocked my wretched being with their glee.

Prone, on despairing knee, I raised my prayer,
   Imploring pity from the shining throng,
Who glided brightly 'round me everywhere,
   On kindly mission, and with thankful song.

Think ye they heard me?   In such happy lot,
   What could they know of misery like mine?
They saw not, heard not—utterly forgot
   Anew I felt the weight of wrath divine.

But, in *one* life, 'twere vain to tell such curse—
   The pangs by which my tortued soul was wrung:—
As well might man crowd back the universe,
   Into the nothingness from which it sprung!

Long had all hopes and strivings, that belong
   . To beings yet the object of God's care,
Been still: the *ages* dragged their length along,
   And yet all hope lay slumb'ring in despair.

When list! a voice of sweetest melody,
  In rapt'rous measure breaks upon my ear,
And nearer comes! Oh joy! it speaks *to me*—
  Oh! wondrous joy!—it utters *words of cheer.*

It bids me rouse my drooping, fainting heart,
  Above its grief, to aspirations pure:—
To live among my kind and do my part,
  And win a happiness that shall endure.

It tells me that the greatness of my crime
  Was trusting *self alone* in trial's hour,
Forgetful of the One who, through all time,
  Has proved Himself the *only source of pow'r.*

It wooes me back to life; again I hear
  The cherished voices of the friends of youth;
And mingle with the forms my heart held dear,
  In the blest hours of infancy and truth;

And bless our Father that the little gleam
  Of what his just and holy wrath *might* be,
Was but a fancy wild—a haunting dream—
  Sent down in boundless love to vanquish me.

And humbly, now, with penitence, I bow
  My chastened will to thine, oh! Holy One!
My dearest wish, *to be pure—e'en as Thou*;—
  My loftiest prayer—*Thy* will, not *mine* be done!

Thou sacred Dove! Come, fold thy peaceful wings,
  And let me ever feel this blissful rest!
Saved,—saved—at last, from those dark wanderings,
  No earthly pow'r can tear Thee from my breast.

Let matchless honors cluster 'round thy throne!
  ·Let hills and vales untiring shout thy praise!
Let earth and ocean cease their strifes, and own
  Thy pow'r and majesty in rapt'rous lays.

Praise Him, ye countless worlds! ye orbs of light
  To him your loftiest hosannas raise!
Awake! ye suns and systems! and unite
  In one harmonious anthem to his praise!

Praise Him, my soul! when wasted skies grow dim,
  And robe their glory in eternal night.
Praise Him my soul! beloved and saved by Him—
  Swell praises to his glory, grace and might!

Ye angels! strike your golden harps anew!

    Let joyful praises gladden your abode!

Teach me the songs that best shall praise Him too,

    Through all the endless ages of our God!

JUNE 1864.

THE THOUGHT THAT CLINGS.

There's gladness in the thought of home,
　'Tis felt, go where we will;
The cradle spot, where'er we roam,
　Hath blessing for us still.
Some old, familiar note of bird,
　Whose echoes 'round us flow,
Reminds us of the songs we heard,
　Far in the long ago:
Of birds that in the window sung,
　With glad hearts, all the day;
Or, wild, among the branches swung,
　Above us, while at play.

The dying, golden autumn leaves
　Come softly rustling down,
And earth, now bright and beautiful,
　Will soon be sere and brown.
And, through the mellow, purple haze,
　A picture dim is seen,

Of other Indian summer days,
　　When life was yet serene;
And children's voices warble out
　　Their dear, familiar chime;
And we are joining in the shout,
　　As in the olden time.

We shut the doors at eventide,
　　And seek the cheering blaze,
And think about the ingleside
　　We sought in younger days:
We trace the pictures in the coals,
　　With sad and thoughtful brow,
And think of hopes we dreamed of *then*,—
　　All dust and ashes *now!*

And silently along we dream,
　　Till all the forms that blest
The days when life was brightest, seem
　　To come at our behest.

Again we're gathered 'round the fire,
　　As in the time of old;
And childish sport beguiles the hour,
　　And fairy tales are told.

And, though a thousand times Grandma,
  In fondness, tell them o'er,
We're just as pleased with them as though
  They'd ne'er been heard before.
A mother's love, upon our mirth,
  Beams like a holy light,
To warn us from the sin of earth,
  And win us to the right.

And now the evening's sport is hushed,
  As, from the sacred page,
A father reads the precious words,
  Which ruled his youth and age.
The rising hymn, in harmony,
  Speaks praise and gladness there;
And then, with reverence, we kneel,
  In humble, earnest prayer.
And then the goodnight kiss is pressed
  Upon each youthful brow,
By lips, to us, immortal *then*—
  All dust and ashes *now!*

Thus on we dream, as trifles bring
　Again the mystic past;
And hallowed mem'ries 'round us cling,
　Of joys too sweet to last.
We mingle with the forms that blest
　The homes that erst we knew;
Or list their spirits wooing us,
　To one *almost in view.*
Ah! sweet, if we could ever live
　Our trusting childhood o'er!
Yet sad, if earth held *all* our joy,
　And Heaven had nothing more!

Oct. '63.

DECORATION DAY.

All honor to the fallen brave—
   With lofty pæans greet the dead!
Let garlands wreathe each lowly grave!
   Let laurel crown each honored head!
'Mid shot and shell, and sabre stroke,
   They bore our colors through the strife,
Till stricken, 'mid the battle smoke,
   They died, to save our country's life!

Though angry skies in blackness bent,
   And shook the shrinking world in wrath;
Though lurid lightnings madly spent
   Their unchained fury in their path:
Through wilderness of woven pine,
   Through slimy pool, and tangled briar,
They marched, in brave, unbroken line,
   Or sunk beneath the clogging mire!

O'er scorching rocks that cut their feet—
　　In hospital, and prison-pen—
Some sank with hunger, thirst and heat,
　　But died no less like patriot-men!
Though spices may not wrap our dead,
　　Nor lofty pyramid arise,
Where justice triumphed while they bled—
　　Their names breathe incense to the skies!

"Dust" may "return to dust," but deep
　　Within the hearts of Freedom's sons,
Embalmed forever, Love shall keep
　　The mem'ry of these faithful ones!
And coming years shall swell our lays,
　　And weave new laurels for each head,
While grateful freeman shout the praise,
　　And glory of COLUMBIA'S DEAD!

THE HAPPY PAST.

Would I might recall the moments
    Of· the precious, fading past;
Would the glorious vision ever
    Might around me last!
Would the same fond eyes, upon me,
    Might their gentle radiance shed—
Would that gentle mother's blessing
    Still might fall upon my head.

Eyes that ever beamed with kindness,
    Lips that oft have pressed my brow—
Loving hearts—lie cold and crumbling
    In the damp earth now.
And the blinding, burning teardrops,
    From my weary spirit start,
As dear Mem'ry's lights and shadows
    Flit across my lonely heart.

Other eyes may smile upon me—
  Hearts as warm be all my own;
But a love that's holier, lingers
  For the angel flown.
When this weary life is ended,
  And death's twilight shadows come,
May that spirit, pure and glorious,
  Be the one to bear me home.

FRAGMENT.

Should we murmur, if our Father,
  In His boundless love hath giv'n
Fire to burn the dross, and brighten
  All that's good in us, for Heav'n?

POEM

Delivered at New England Dinner, Marshall, Mich. 1871.

Away, for awhile, from life's wearisome conflict,
  On furlough, we haste to this banquet of cheer;
The love of New England, our hale-hearted mother,
  The bond that unites us, and gathers us here.

And blest is this board, with its joy overflowing!
  No feast of the gods yielded gladness so sweet
As this, while, with tasks laid aside for a season.
  'Round the table fraternal, like children, we meet.

Only *grand*-children, some, with more fancy than
      mem'ry
  Of grandmother's manners, time-honored and
      quaint;
Her face, even, strange, or at best but a glimmer,
  That flits through our dreams but uncertain and
      faint.

Very wise was New England, when settling her
　　children !—

With the tact of a Chieftain, she gathered her *best*,

And bade them go forth to their war with the forests

　　And people and gladden this beautiful *West!*

And peopled it was, till her prairies were gardens,

　　And cities sprang up in the arms of the wild;

And New England, astonished, with the silence of
　　wisdom,

　　Took a seat in the lap of her overgrown child!

A strange, loving child, with its mother's hale virtues,

　　Though the noise in its speech disturbs all of her
　　　nerves,

A revenue yields her of valleys unmeasured,

　　And the government too with a few wise reserves.

Dear glorious land! from the gray rock of Plymouth,

　　Afar to the gold-gleaming slope of the West,

Thy children are brothers, thou *all* art New England,

　　For the strong heart of Liberty thorbs in each
　　　breast.

The morn of thy youth is obscured in thy brightness,

But oh ! for the future we fain would forecast,

While Pride and Ambition embrace even Error,

Nor dream of a transport too perfect to last!

Years crowd upon years, like the foam crested breakers,

That beat on the beautiful, sand-drifted shore;

They wear down the pictures that seem to us sacred,

And soon they must cheer even mem'ry no more !

Dim—dimmer than dreams, come the deeds of Miles Standish,

'Mid the hurry and worry and glare of to day;

And a myth is the cot where Priscilla sat spinning,

Till Raghorn, the beautiful, bore her away!

Yet far 'mid those hills, there's a cottage as lowly,

Where "mother's" sweet voice to the spinning wheel sung;

And here, in our midst, there are *sons* of John Alden,

With hearts as heroic as his whence they sprung!

How oft have we gathered around the old fireside,
   In times that grow sacred, with gathering years!
The visions of lang syne arise, rainbow-tinted,
   To us, as we view them through fast rising tears!

And fond recollection shall pause at *this* meeting,
   While counting her gems, as the daylight departs:
We'll put it away, with the mem'ry of mother,
   And childhood's glad orisons, deep in our hearts.

Oh! blest be the bond of bright years that unites us,
   For life has no meed like the love of the true;
No gift of the throng e'er so sweetly requites us,
   Or nerves us so bravely to dare and to do.

And meet though the honors we yield to the heroes,
   Who labor among us, a Heaven blest band;
Yet riper and richer shall circle the mem'ry
   Of those who first opened the doors of our land!

A VOICE FROM THE RANKS.

Written and delivered at the request of the "Ladies' Temperance League," August 1874.

Fair was the world, to outward eyes,
    And joy awoke the laggard Spring;
The sun looked down from azure skies,
    And kissed the robin's russet wing.

The signal sounds, so often giv'n,
    Were lost upon the reckless air:
We only caught the smiles of Heav'n,
    Though Sin trode raging in his lair.

And spirits, from the lower deep,
    By midnight wandered to and fro;
Their orgies rose above our sleep,
    Like echoes from the world of woe.

Their nets they spread, in street and lane;
　　In every path, their snares they wove:
With madness hushed their victim's pain,
　　As, helpless, in their toils he strove.

For avarice, with blinding spell,
　　Won to their aid man's cunning hand;
And Peace rang out her parting knell,
　　As Honor fled the blighted land.

The grey-haired father calmly went
　　His daily path, with trusting tread;
With years of noble deeds, low bent,
　　That crowned with joy his hoary head.

Love searched for him till evening fall—
　　She wearied not when midnight came;
The withered frame, she found, but all
　　The better part was lost in shame.

The man of strength went forth in hope,
　　To toil, of danger unaware—
At eve, alas! we saw him grope,
　　Blind, helpless in the fatal snare.

The loving mother rose, at morn,
  With blessings for each dear one's head;
Her fingers fain would pluck each thorn
  From out the path their feet must tread.

That noble son, with soul that viewed
  The field of manhood just before—
How bright the scene, and golden-hued!—
  How full the grain, and rich in store!

Alas! for hopes on earth reposed!
  Alas! for love that clings to clay!
The fatal toils around him closed,
  And grief eclipsed the glowing day!

That little one with floating hair,
  And dimpled beauty, pure and sweet—
Ah! *surely* loving Heav'n, with care,
  Will ever guard *her* guileless feet.

Bright, mocking hope! why falsely sing?
  Who doth the fatal winecup spare?
The lovliest feel its hidden sting—
  None are too pure, and none too fair.

The careworn face, the drooping eye,
  Too soon bespeak the blighted life:
Her singing hushes to a sigh—
  Alas!—she is a drunkard's wife!

And mother hearts that should have kept
  The ward of paths where dangers teem,
At gate or helm or doorway slept,
  Or, waking, walked as in a dream.

But list! there comes a sound of war—
  The air is full of strange alarms;
We catch the bugle note afar,
  And waking, wildly fly to arms!

Ah! now the startled foe appears,
  We rally for the thick'ning strife;
By Love inspired, adieu! to fears—
  We come with *consecrated life.*

No passing whim, of moment's length,
  Beguiled us to this mortal fight;
Our grief is deep, and small our strength,
  But *God* is ours, and He is MIGHT!

With humble faith we seek his will—
　We meet Him, heart to heart, in prayer;
And, though He slay us, trust Him still.
　And cast on Him our crushing care.

Our plodding toil of patient days
　Shall end in gladness, by and by;
Our waiting souls shall see the blaze
　Of God's unfailing victory.

We work with Him, we wait His hour,
　Nor dream of weariness or rest;
The souls we love are in our pow'r—
　'Tis *that*, inspires each shrinking breast.

Go learn the pangs our darlings feel,
　That drunkards' wives and mothers know—
Ye then may guess that nerves of steel
　May live beneath a gentle brow.

The passing child may thrill with fear
　The timid breast of wildwood dove,
Till, only from afar, we hear
　Her tender coo, and song of love.

But let the serpent's slimy form
    Disturb her brood—invade her nest—
Her mother-love subdues alarm,
    And courage nerves her downy breast.

A frenzied rage, her will inspires,
    Her cries, her agony bespeak,
Her nestling's peril swiftly fires
    Her beating wings, and tearing beak.

And mother birds, from far and near,
    Of every song, and every plume,
Her frantic shrieks of vengeance, hear,
    And fly to seal the monster's doom.

With head upraised in venomed pride,
    And folds that writhe in subtle strength,
With lulling charm, they see him glide,
    And slow uncoil his fearful length.

Transfixed and silently await
    The helpless birdlings, in the nest.
Ah! what shall stay impending fate,
    Or guard the shrieking mother's breast!

And now the combat wages hot—
  'Tis poison fang 'gainst beak and wing,
The fallen few are heeded not
  By those who parry, coil and sting.

And still they close, till, one by one,
  The valiant parent birds are slain;
And oft, before the fight is done,
  But few of that first flock remain.

But *other* birds, from quiet haunts,
  Into the ranks have softly flown,
With courage which no horror daunts,
  And made the cause of right, their own.

No time have they to chirp their grief
  O'er fallen ones, that 'neath them lie;
Or tremble with the dire belief
  That, if they fight, they too must die.

Their quenchless *will*, the serpent feels,
  And sinks beneath the ceaseless strife;
And, wounded, fainting, dying—seals
  The rightful triumph with his life.

Then, upward from the victor flock,
   A peal of gladness rends the sky;
And valley sweetly answers rock,
   In tuneful song of VICTORY!

Within the quiet haunts of home,
   Frail woman sought and loved repose:
She had no will or wish to roam,
   Or try her unskilled hand with foes.

When sorrows came she could not cure,
   In time they sighed themselves to rest:
She did not vanquish, but endure,
   And hoarded strength within her breast.

But some there were who sorrow knew,
   Too dark for speech, too deep for tears—
It touched them and their children too,
   And blighted all their after years.

They saw their loved, the weak, the strong,
　The young, the beautiful, the brave,
Join, daily, in the frenzied throng,
　That rushes to a drunkard's grave.

To stay the doom so justly feared,
　With man we plead for better laws;
He heard and labored, till appeared
　A faultless statute for our cause.

We onward floated then awhile,
　With thankful souls, and hope elate:
We, long before, had learned to toil—
　We now alas! must learn to *wait!*

The men who framed that statute fair.
　In silence, slept a score of years,
Unmoved by the inebriate's prayer,
　And stricken woman's grief and tears.

For Avarice, with orient charm,
　Touched loving hearts and turned them
　　stone—
Unaided by each nerveless arm,
　We grappled with the foe *alone.*

If from the strong no help may come,
　　If madness lure them from our side,
Till *we are forced to fight for home*,
　　It ill becomes them now to chide!

From cowardice and greed awake!
　　Put holy laws into effect—
No more the sacred promise break,
　　"To love, to cherish and *protect!*"

Then see how swiftly home we'll turn,
　　As wearied birdling seeks her nest;.
Our Vestal fires shall brighter burn,
　　And Love re'wakened, flood each breast.

But, as we meet in clashing fray,
　　Our loved to save, our homes to free.
No sneers or jesting shall dismay,
　　For *Duty* is "*propriety.*"

'Tis love that reigns in woman's breast—
　　Love lifts and nerves her puny hand:
'Twas danger to her dear home nest,
　　That first her flick'ring courage fanned.

The weakness of her finer frame,
 She supplements by faith and will,
That soon shall put to flight and shame,
 The deadly "serpent of the still."

His coil he throws across our path—
 In sullen strength he lifts his head—
With forked tongue he hisses wrath,
 And gloats in triumph o'er the dead.

And some who know his subtle charm,
 . His grasp of steel, his gleaming eye—
Before his threat'ning take alarm,
 And, lost to love and honor, fly.

And some, in utter weariness,
 Have fainted, though they did not yield:
Their faith, their prayers are ours no less,
 Though forced awhile to quit the field.

The serpent grew, by vict'ry bold—
 Vile calumny on some he flung:
For some, the boughs that bore them gold,
 In malice he adroitly stung.

Then up to Heav'n, with hearts that ache,
 We breathe our loss, for God hath said —
"The righteous I will not forsake —
 Their children shall not want for bread."

As angry clouds, at morn unfurled,
 With glory gild the waning day,
So cometh gladness that the world
 Can neither give nor take away.

In memory, we hear the tones
 Of some, once foremost in the fray;
Their hearts are writhing for their sons —
 What *can* their longing footsteps stay?

Alas! that home should ever be
 What many homes to women are! —
Where Patience sighs for liberty,
 Behind a golden bolt and bar!

To live, and live uncomforted,
 With fettered hands, with pleasure flown,
Where passing years once lightly sped,
 They learn, and weep and pray *alone*.

With silent lips they bear their grief;
  With sacred trust their vows they keep;
So, tortured, bound, with no relief,
  What can they do but pray and weep?

But furrows steal upon their cheeks,
  And circles shade their drooping eyes;
Thus Grief her saddest language speaks,
  While hushing e'en her softest sighs!

God wearies not, and He can see,
  And gather all our tears that rise:
By Love illumined, they shall be
  A pearly pathway to the skies!

And, o'er its radiant arches, swift
  Our prayers shall glide, with wingéd feet;
God shall the cloudy curtain lift—
  His love, our sad petitions greet!

But though, by flight, or weariness,
  Or silken fetters, deftly bound,
We've sometimes seen our ranks grow less,
  Some sure relief was always found.

In quiet homes, through all the land,
  Is heard each signal of distress,
And help appears—another band—
  And to the battle front *they* press.

Again and yet again they rise—
  This combat shows a wondrous length;
For God commands us, from the skies,
  And he inspires our garnered strength.

With faith unshaken, on we move,
  Unshrinking till the fight is past;
Our will, unwav'ring as our love!
  Shall welcome victory at last.

And when, in death, the monster, fell,
  Lies stretched upon the plain below,
A myriad mother hearts shall swell,
  With songs of gladness o'er the foe!

Praise God! shall through the valley ring;
  Praise God! shall echo through the sky;
And orisons of gladness wing,
  To God, who giveth victory!

To-day, that anthem might begin,
    If men, who bear the saviour's name,
Would rise against this deadly sin,
    Nor longer put their vows to shame.

Ring not these Heav'nly accents still?—
    "Not every one that *saith* Lord, Lord,
But *he that* DOTH *my Father's will*,
    Shall hear, at last, the welcome word."

What *is* his will? What do we mean,
    When praying "let thy will be done?"
Is it that earth should be a scene
    Of blackest crime, from sun to sun?

Is it that day and night astound
    The pow'rs below, with groans and tears?
Is it that you, their fearful sound,
    Let fall *unheeded* on your ears?

Oh Life! Oh Love! lift up your cries,
    Till thoughtless, dreaming men awake;
Or wrath will burst the patient skies,
    And heads must bow, and hearts must break!

Pause from the chase for worthless things—
　For pleasure, dying with the day;
And gold that only taketh wings,
　And, ere we know it, flits away.

Is gold real riches? Should it be
　That you had only daily bread,
Would you not be as rich as he
　Who had "not where to lay his head?"

List to the words by Heaven sealed—
　Uttered by Him who knew no sin:
"Behold the lilies of the field,
　They toil not, neither do they spin,

Yet Solomon, in all his state,
　Was not arrayed like one of these:—
Ye faithless! dearer far your fate,
　To him, than lilies in the breeze!"

Seek first the righteousness of God,
　And He shall add sufficient store;
Follow the path by Jesus trod,
　And never thirst or hunger more!

How *dare* ye pray "Thy will be done,"
　　While, by your suff'rance, vice is free,
And souls to ruin hurry on?—
　　Will Heaven brook such mockery?

Your wordy prayers, like poisoned spears,
　　Shall *pierce* you in the judgment day;
Insulted Truth will scorn your tears—
　　Too late to work—too late to pray!

Upon your brows the mark of Cain
　　Is set by an offended God!
Depart! no more his board profane,
　　Till ye are cleansed in Jesus' blood!

What though your temples, towering
　　Their gilded spires, reach up to Heav'n!
God loveth not the gift you bring;—
　　The "*price of blood*" is for it giv'n!

Go, take the price of *sob* and *sigh*—
　　Of *souls*, forever lost in sin—
Take it, ye hypocrites! and buy
　　"A field to bury strangers in!"

A few there are, a faithful few,
　　Who follow in their Master's tread;
True to themselves, to Heaven true—
　　God's love defend each honored head!

The clutch of Crime upon the land,
　　With holy wrath, their spirits fired:
No threat could daunt, no foe withstand,
　　For Duty led, and Faith inspired!

By patient labor, have they shown
　　Their fealty to their risen Lord;
Their pow'r is felt, their work is known,
　　Where Right once languished and implored.

Toil on, ye brave! God reigneth still!
　　He sees you weep, He hears you sigh:
The clouds that darken vale and hill,
　　Shall break, in gladness, by and by!

As, in the dim, azoic past,
　　Broad continents in silence lay—
Their wealth and beauty cloud o'ercast,
　　Awaiting the approaching day:

So sleeps, to-day, the moral world,
In clouds of ignorance and sin;
Her wealth unused, her beauty furled,
Till God's bright day is ushered in!

Roll on, ye hours! Roll on, ye years!
Till breaks the morn our hopes forecast:
Of small account, our toils and tears,
Beside the joy that comes at last!

Father! to Thee we lift our eyes;
Thou art our hope, our strength, our all:
Thy love shall listen to our cries—
It noteth e'en the sparrow's fall.

The way is dark and rough and long;
Our hearts are faint, our feet are sore;
We cheer its devious length with song,
For Christ has walked the path before.

No anguish for another's sin—
No agony our spirits know,
From foes without, or foes within,
But *He* hath felt it *long ago.*

With humble rev'rence, we pursue
  The bright example he hath giv'n;
Rejoiced to know the grief He knew,
  And share, with Him, the bliss of Heav'n.

Oh! may we never once forget
  The blood for *us* so *freely* spilt;
The midnight groans, and crimson sweat
  That plead with God for sinners' guilt!

Dear Saviour! what hast thou not borne,
  Of toil and pain and infamy?
Then welcome! labor, sorrow, scorn—
  'Tis all for Thee—dear Christ—for thee!

Increase our courage, rouse our faith,
  To visions of the promised land;
Nor ever let us lose, till death,
  Our hold upon thy guiding hand!

Father, forgive the thoughtlessness
  Of those who fain would honor Thee,
Whom smaller sins of men oppress,
  While this great crime they do not see.

Forgive, and rouse them, by thy love,
  To humbly ask and work they will;
By action, deep repentance prove;
  By sacrifice, thy law fulfil.

Help them to love and succour those
  Who love them not again: to find
Mercy, not only for their foes,
  But for the helpless, halt and blind.

Father, stretch forth thy mighty arm,
  For thou, alone, hast pow'r to save
The victims of the winecup's charm,
  And ward them from a drunkard's grave.

With giddy steps, from year to year,
  The wild procession hurries on—
Too gay to pause, too proud to fear,
  Till o'er the horrid steep they're gone.

The old and trembling, and the strong,
  The bridegroom, and his gentle bride,
And tender childhood, swell the song
  And surging of this living tide.

Sometimes the syren's spell is lost
   A moment, and the truth appears;
Then, oh! how full they pay the cost
   Of mocking mirth, in heart wrung tears!

The hungry cries of little ones—
   The tear of shame, in loving eyes,—
The downward steps of watchful sons—
   The scorn of all whose love they prize;—

Health, pleasure, hope and honor fled—
   A bankrupt name, a ruined home,
Where, (souls and bodies well nigh dead,)
   Like dread, disfigured ghosts they come:—

These are the winning wine-cup's price,
   With souls aghast, they waking see:
Oh! how they loathe their clinging vice!—
   How madly struggle to be free!

Too late, alas! their toil is vain,
   For wine hath robbed them of their will;
No pow'rs remain to burst the chain;
   The links but tighten 'round them still.

Then trembling, sinking in despair,
   They walk the earth no more like men:
In madness seek to banish care,
   And sink beneath the brutes again.

Or, with a sense of helplessness,
   That feels not e'en God's pow'r to save,
What wonder, some, from deep distress,
   Seek peaceful refuge, *in the grave!*

Kind Heaven! spare them from that hour;
   With holy balm, their spirits heal:
No miracle exceeds thy pow'r—
   The lowest may thy mercy feel.

Come! wingéd messengers of light!
   And whisper of the crucified;
With heavenly morning banish night—
   It was *for sinners Jesus died!*

Soft fall the shades, at eventide;
　The starlight glistens on the dew;
The robin trills, her nest beside,
　Her song of love, forever new.

And songs of love, from happy hearts.
　Rise, where the ruddy lamplight glows;
For peace descends, as day departs,
　And home her sweetest gladness knows.

Papa, with forehead crossed by care,
　Sits down, for respite, with a smile:
And, from his ample easy chair,
　Perchance some fragment reads, the while.

Adieu! anxiety and toil!
　And welcome! moments love-caressed!
With romp and game the hours beguile,
　For rest is bliss, and these are rest!

The little ones, with tameless mirth,
　Their small feet patter to and fro;
Believing life's chief end, on earth,
　Is "Blind man's buff" or "Children go."

While older ones with head inclined,
　With earnest eye, and lip sedate,
By patient study, smile to find
　A mine of wealth in book and slate.

The happy mother sings to sleep
　The sweet one pillowed on her breast,
With soft caress that fain would keep
　Her darling from his cradlenest.

And then the Holy Book is brought,
　And words of love and guidance read;
Forgiveness for the past is sought,
　And blessing for each waiting head.

And then the soft "good nights" are heard,
　And childhood's slumbers quickly come:
But waiting still, with loving word,
　The busy mother haunts the room.

She bends above their snowy bed,
　And heav'nly sweetness fills her eyes;
She softly strokes each silken head,
　And smiles to hear their drowsy sighs.

Their very breathing, music seems,
  And fairer theirs than cherub's cheek:
Her loving whispers gild their dreams;
  Her glist'ning eyes her bliss bespeak.

Fond mother, when, safe here at home,
  You hover o'er their slumbers sweet,
Do never dark forebodings come,
  Of. pitfalls for their tender feet?

Dost never think, when thrilled with fear,
  By drunken shoutings, coarse and wild—
The poor outcast, whose voice you hear,
  Was once a mother's sinless child?

At night, she bent above his bed,
  With fond caresses for his cheek—
Breathed blessings on his sunny head,
  And wept the love she could not speak.

Stay, wingéd Time, thy journey fleet—
  While peace and joy like this we know!
Thy pinions fold!—too rich, too sweet
  These precious hours, to let them go!

Yes, sweet to find our loved at home,
   When laggard sunset flies the hill;
When midnight's dark temptations come,
   To know our love may guard them still.

Kind Heaven, can the future prove
   A morn like theirs must set in gloom?
Is there no pow'r in all our love,
   To shield them from a drunkard's doom?

To godly fear their hearts we train,
   With filial love their aims inspire;
Each baser thought with care restrain,
   And early guard each pure desire.

The world we search for highest arts—
   Bring gems and sculptured offerings,
And everything that joy imparts,
   That knowledge gives, or pleasure brings.

We fill our homes with young and gay;
   Of harmless joys they drink their fill;
And *yet* their guarded feet will stray—
   The fatal wine-cup lures them *still!*

What wonder, when, on every street
  And step, Hell keeps a gilded gate;
And, for their unsuspecting feet,
  The patient devils mask and wait?

Oh! that such sins of men might stain
  'Th' offenders brow to Ethiop hue:
And souls, where godlike virtues reign,
  Might let their heav'nly radiance through!

Then might the guileless flee aghast,
  In quick disgust, the tempter's smile;
And purer friends, and joys that last,
  In heav'nly guise, their steps beguile.

These dens are in the paths to toil,
  To churches, business, games and schools;
And *music* drowns their fiendish broil,
  While Reason sleeps, and Passion rules.

Their owners look like better men;
  Their brows are mild, their voices kind;
And so friends drink and call again,
  To art and danger ever blind.

But Shame the scepter will assume—
   Shame finds new names for infamy:
The beer saloon's a "Sample Room,"
   The whiskey shop, a "Grocery."

Shame paints their signs, and builds their
     screens,
   And dims their windows half way up:
By day and night enacts her scenes,
   And bends abandoned o'er the cup.

By Shame, proud sums of gold, ill-won,
   Upon the church's shrine is laid;
As though such off'rings could atone
   For guileless souls enticed—betrayed!

Still unreleased by Shylock-Shame,
   Their plans they change, for future years:
Their lives, they say, shall baffle blame,
   And *alms* atone for orphans' tears.

But stronger grows their thirst for gold;
   And fainter rise their nobler aims;
Till hope is lost in pangs untold,
   And Death the vile decoyer claims.

Oh! boundless Love that stooped to touch
   The leper, in his foul distress,
Unveil thy winning face to such,
   And woo their cursing lips to bless!

We see them leading souls to death,
   Unconscious that *their footsteps too*
Are rushing down the *same dark path*,
   And *they* must *share* their victims' wo.

We call to them, in gentlest tones;
   They heed us only while we speak:
Again we plead, while urged by moans,
   From hearts that writhe and bleed and break.

We point them up to purer joys—
   To paths that lead to Paradise:
They answer us in jesting voice,
   Or stupid leer of bloodshot eyes.

Oh God! we murmur, can it be
   That souls like these can *never die?*
If unforgiv'n, can never flee
   The fire of thy pursuing eye?

Must bear the curse of souls undone,
　The souls of those *their crimes destroyed*—
Shut out from bliss they might have won—
　Decoyers by themselves decoyed?

And this forever! Bend we low:
　This thought a flood wave o'er us rolls!
For them, thou God *alone* canst know
　The anguish of our pleading souls!

Would they might see, above them, hung
　The bolts of thy suspended wrath!
The mutt'ring clouds around them flung,
　Must burst in vengeance on their path!

We feel the uselessness of all
　Our words and tears, and, led by Thee,
And trusting Thee, on law we call,
　And work and wait for victory.

"Save *them*, oh! save them!" still we cry,
　While forcing them the young to spare;
Our souls' desire must pierce the sky—
　Thou art a God that hearest prayer!

Though conscience, palsied and confined,
   Scarce murmurs in her restless sleep;
Though souls are numb and deaf and blind,
   And eyes long since unused to weep:

Where'er the faintest germ of life,
   That reaches God-ward, still is left,
In souls with evil passions rife,
   Of hope and will, almost bereft—

Within their chambers, dark and close,
   Breathe living warmth, from heav'nly fire;
Let nought the swelling germ oppose,
   Or check the growth of pure desire.

So shall thine image grow at last,
   From out each wearied, sinscarred soul;
Till, at thy feet, his all is cast,
   And Mercy whispers "Be thou whole!"

But is there one so hard, so base,
   He *ne'er* will heed thy Spirits' call,
For whom remains *no day of grace*—
   On him, let Heav'n's swift vengeance fall!

Why should he stay but to destroy?
　Why fetters forge for pure and free?
Long life can neither bring him joy,
　Nor shorten his eternity!

Death's messengers, at every hand,
　With ready feet, await thy nod;
Then why should such thy cause withstand,
　Defying man, insulting God!

In *pity*, loving Heav'n remove
　These hindrances from out Thy way;
And spare the children of our love,
　From human demons, such as they!

Dear sisters, God will hear our prayers,
　Will save our land from wine, accurs'd,
Though we may leave these heavy cares,
　And climb the shining stairway *first*.

The patient Lord of earth and sky,
　Who bore our griefs, and for us died,
Saw, only with prophetic eye,
　The good for which he worked and sighed.

So let our patience grow like His;
　　So let us labor, sorrow, die;
So may we trust God's promises,
　　And see the end through Faith's clear eye!

Then, when awakes the solemn day,
　　That seals our actions, bad or good,
We'll hear the voice of Jesus say—
　　Sweet words—"She hath done what she
　　could!"

SONGS.

AWAY TO THE SILVER-LIT SEA.

Away! while the white moon is beaming—
    Away! to the silver-lit sea!
While the dew laden flowers are dreaming,
    Come, Winnie, come darling with me.
To thy song shall the nightingale listen,
    And the wild breezes slumber for thee;
While thy voice shall the mystic harps waken,
    'Neath the swell of the silver-lit sea!

CHORUS—

      Beautiful, beautiful Winnie—
        Beautiful ever to me—
      But never so beautiful, darling,
        As to-night, on the silver-lit sea!

Oh! sweet are the voices that love us,
    When heard at the dear ingleside;
But sweeter, with moonlight above us,
    As we float on the swell of the tide.

How tenderly, softly they echo,
    The beat of the waves on the shore—
Like memories cherished and golden,
    Of sweet, faded summers of yore!

CHORUS.

Oh! brightly thy drooping eyes glisten
    The love that thy lips will not speak;
I feel thou art mine while I listen,
    And see the rose bloom on thy cheek.
Thus ever, my darling, forever,
    I'd float on life's billow with thee—
Thy dear voice forever awaking
    Its sweet mystic music for me!

CHORUS,

GREETING SONG.

*For the Quinquennial reunion of the Atheniades' Society of
Albion College, April 25th, 1870.*

With chorus of greeting we welcome you all,
　　To our circle of hearts, warm and true;
Let no thought divide us, who come at this call,
　　To the home where our old friendship grew.

CHORUS—

　　And brothers and sisters, let this be our song,
　　Forever—come weal or come woe—
　　There are no friends like the good old friends
　　That we loved in the long ago!

We've stood by each other, for many a year,
　　Whether sunshine or storm filled the sky;
　Each had, for the others, some word of good cheer,
　　Though Hope spread her pinions to fly.

　　　　　　Then brothers and sisters, etc.

Long years, a frail craft, were we tossed by the sea,
    But the old motto * blazed like the sun;
And we clung to the ship, for we knew it must be,
    That our voyage was only begun.
            Then brothers and sisters, etc.

Now flaunt thy bright pennon, and set ev'ry sail,
    For proudly, at length, mayst thou ride:
'Neath thy beauty is strength, that can weather the
    gale,
    And skill, that can baffle the tide!
            Then brothers and sisters, etc.

*Nunquam da navem.

NEVER FEAR MOLLY, OR ALL FOR THIS CHILLY, DRIVING RAIN.

Oh! the night is dark and dreary, and the rain be-
gins to fall,
And it was to-night, you know, mamma, that Willie
said he'd call;
But there's no use list'ning longer, for he wont be
here at all, .
And all for this chilly, driving rain! rain! rain!

CHORUS—

Oh! never fear a moment, Molly darling, don't you
know, .
There never was a hurricane, of lightning hail or
snow,
Or of harder things I've heard of, but through it man
would go,
If the girl he loved sat waiting, with her heart, like
yours, aglow.

It may be he had started before the rain began—

But, if so, he'll spend the evening with that hateful Sary Ann,

For she lives full two blocks nearer, and she'll stop him, if she can,

And all for this chilly, driving rain! rain! rain!

CHORUS.

But hark! I hear a footstep, and the swinging of the gate—

I surely thought it later—why, it has not yet struck eight!

Oh! Willie! is it you? I was sure at home you'd wait,

When the night brought this chilly, driving rain! rain! rain!

CHORUS.

Oh! never fear, a moment, Molly darling, don't you know

There never was a hurricane, of lightning, hail or snow,

Or of pitchforks or of grindstones, but through it man would go,

· If the girl he loved sat waiting, with her heart like yours aglow.

A TRIBUTE TO THE MENNONITES.

In the south hills of Russia, there dwelt a brave
band;

The true, sturdy sons of the dear father-land;

Each with God-loving heart, and with toil hardened
hand;

And they planted the olive and vine:

Fair little ones played 'round each cottager's door;

And blest was the hamlet, in health and in store;

And they worshipped their God, as they worshipped
of yore,

When they dwelt on the banks of the Rhine.

CHORUS—

All hail! to the heroes of seventy-four,

Let their names be enrolled with the heroes of
yore,

Whom, to rocky New England, the Mayflower
bore,

For Freedom to worship God!

But the time honored cross of the iron-browed Czar,

Could brook not the heresy heard from afar,

But, by fetters and fire, and the terrors of war,

  Peace pined in that hamlet, and died.

Then, away from the friends that they loved in good
     sooth,

From the graves of their sires, and the homes of
     their youth,

They went, for the honor of God, and of truth,

  And America's arms opened wide.

CHORUS.

Ever mild shall the skies be that over them shine;

Like gold be their wheat, and like nectar their wine;

For the Hand that hath led, and shall lead, is Di-
     vine—

  May that dear Hand be ever in view!

And proudly let Freedom her pæans awake,

Let valley and hill into harmony break,

And the wild winds the strain back to fatherland
     take,

  That we sing for the brave and the true!

CHORUS.

"WAITING FOR PAPA."

The night closed in darkness and weeping,
  The rain fell in slow, sullen beat;
The village, I thought, was all sleeping,
  Unheeding the tramp of my feet:
When, soft, as I passed a low portal,
  A sweet, little voice that I knew,
Cried out, in the darkness, "Dear papa!
  You know I am waiting for you!"

CHORUS—

  "Waiting, dear papa! I'm waiting, still waiting—
    You soon would be coming, I knew;
  And moonlight or darkness or tempest or cold,
    I'll nightly be waiting for you!"

The little maid peered through the shadows,
  And sadness stole over her tone;
'Twas not he for whom she, so bravely,
  Stood watching and waiting alone,

She sighed, as I gently caressed her—
   All wet was her soft, clinging hair,
And damp were her garments—I whispered
   "Go in, child, and wait for him there!"

CHORUS.

   "Ah, no!" was her quick, earnest answer,
     "When mama was dying, you know,
She laid her white hand on my forehead
     And told me to wait for him *so:*
And when by the wine he is tempted,
     Of me, *by the gate*, he will think—
The revel no longer remember,
     And so I may save him from drink."

CHORUS.

I left the dear child at the gateway,
   The last of a once sunny home,
And wondered, while braving the tempest,
   How long ere that father would come;
And why, while the hearth is still cheery,
   Men check not their steps to the grave,
Nor wait till the fond hearts grow weary,
   And above them the wild flowers wave.

CHORUS TO LAST VERSE—

Waiting, no longer they're waiting, they're wait-
   ing,
   With hearts beating welcome so true;
And, moonlight or darkness, or tempest or cold,
   'Tis lonely and silent for you.

MARY! SWEET MARY! I DREAM OF THEE, EVER!

Adown in the valley, where wild rose and willow,
  Their bright boughs entwine, o'er the low, limpid
    stream;
I wander, once more, in the day's dying glory,
  And muse on the gladness of life's early dream.
Though autumn has come, and the silver threads
    glisten
  'Mid locks that were jet, in the days of my pride;
Yet sorrow nor years can dispel the fond vision
  Of Mary, the maiden I wooed as my bride!

CHORUS—

    Mary! sweet Mary! I dream of thee ever,
    And weep for the morning to banish my gloom!
      The brightness of earth shall awake for me
      never,
    For the light of my life is all hid in thy tomb!

The gossamer veil, and the soft robes of tissue,
  Enfold her fair form, in her low, silent bed;
And garlands of orange, and sweet, drooping myrtle,
  They 'twined for her bridal, encircle her head.
Adown by the stream, where so oft we had wandered,
  They laid her to rest, where the primroses wave;
I'm weary of waiting so long for the morning—
  My joy is all hushed in the gloom of her grave!

Chorus—

  Mary! sweet Mary! The morning is breaking!
  Already its light is dispelling my gloom!
  I'm coming—I'm coming—all sorrow forsaking,
  To clasp thee, immortal, in God's bright home!

"THE OLD HOMESTEAD TREE."

Far down, in the shadowy valley of years,
    That make up the sweet "long ago,"
There's *one sunny* spot, unbeclouded by tears,
    At rest, in the soft, morning glow.
'Tis the dearly loved home where in childhood
      I played,   •
    And rang out my innocent glee,
While loved ones kept time, with a musical
      chime,
    In the shade of the old, homestead tree.

CHORUS—

  Yes, dear to my heart, sunny mem'ry, thou art;
    May nought thy fond gleam from me sever,
  Of the dear ones who dwelt in that low, shaded
      cot,
    And who loved, and will love me forever!

Beneath its rude branches, dwelt all the dear
forms

That made earth a Heaven appear;

It sheltered our cottage, from sun, and from
storms,

Through many a swift, gliding year.

Till, from out its broad shadow, they went—one
by one—

To a better home, sinless and free;

And left me to wander the wide world alone,

Far away from the old homestead tree.

CHORUS—

Yet dear to my heart, sunny mem'ry, thou art;

May nought thy fond gleam from me sever,

Of the dear ones who dwelt in that low, shaded
cot,

And who loved, and will love me, forever!

Years hurry along, but that dream of the past,

Clings, lovingly, 'round my lone way;

And I know, when with shadows my sky is o'er
cast,

'Tis the darkness that heralds the day.

In that home, whose strange beauty can never-
more fade,
The loved ones are waiting for me;
And they'll waft a sweet welcome to her who
once played
With them, 'neath the old homestead tree.

CHORUS—

Dear, dear to my heart, sunny mem'ry, thou art;
May nought thy fond gleam from me sever,
Of the dear ones who dwelt in that low, shaded
cot,
And who loved, and will love me forever!

SOCIETY GREETING SONG.

With merry, merry lay, we hail this day
   Of glad fraternal meeting;
And welcome true, again renew,
   With song of joyous greeting.
No breath of care shall tinge the air,
   Or tremble in our singing,
But the birds shall wake, and echo make,
   To our merry voices ringing,
To the tra la la la la trala la, la, la,
   Of our merry, merry voices ringing.

The garlands that we bring, their perfume
     fling,
   An incense sweet ascending,
To mem'ries bright, of dear delight,
   Their smiles and fragrance lending.
And love and truth, and hope and youth

Shall triumph in our singing,
Till the birds shall wake and echo make
　　To our merry voices ringing—
To the tra la la la la trala la, la, la,
　　Of our merry, merry voices ringing!

Oh! may each happy year, that brings us here,
　　With joy be overflowing;
And years between, may we be seen,
　　The seeds of gladness, sowing.
Good deeds, alone, the soul can throne,
　　And fill the heart with singing,
Till the birds shall wake, and echo make
　　With a peal of gladness ringing—
To the trala la la la trala la, la, la,
　　Of our merry, merry voices ringing!

SONG OF FREEDOM.

Brothers awake! ere the knell of our country
    Is sounded, and traitors hold sway in the land.
Wake! and come forth in this darkness and peril!
    "Divided we fall"—but "United we stand!"

Shall we, who have gloried in peace and in freedom,
    And wept o'er the chain of the poor, oppressed slave,
Calmly sit down, while they fasten *our* fetters?—
    Sleep? as they bury our *name* in the grave?

Long have we played in the front of their cannon;
    If we play longer, the Nation is lost!
Wake! ere the last hope of liberty perish;
    Think what it is to us! Think what it cost!

Feb. 1863.

SONG OF THE EXILE.

Far in a sunny, southern clime,
   Where sighs the restless sea,
There stands a vine-embowered cot,
   E'en yet that's dear to me.
The elm trees link above the stream,
   Just as they did of yore—
But ah! I would it were a dream,
   I'll wander there no more!

Long years have passed since there I strayed,
   A little child at play;
The light wind sporting with the locks,
   That now are turning gray.
And those who were my playmates then—
   The guileless and the gay,
Whose hearts were full of love, and truth,
   And fond hopes—Where are they?

Sweet mem'ries cling around the spot,
  That once was home to me;
And still I love to live again
  The days that used to be.
Time has estranged, and sadly chilled
  The hearts I thought my own;
And, in my few short exile years,
  I've strangely weary grown.

They've been so full of bitterness,
  ·I would they were a dream,
And I might once again awake,
  Beside that mountain stream;
And find the world as good and pure
  As it is bright and fair;
Then lay me down—while yet a child,
  And breathe my life out there!

1858 SUMMER.

TEMPERANCE ARMY SONG.

TUNE—"JOHN BROWN."

Our souls shall see the triumph of the army of the
Lord!

He'll hear our cry of agony, He's promised in his
Word;—

Intemperance shall perish, by the Christian woman's
sword,

And victory is nigh!

CHORUS—

Glory, glory, hallelujah!

Glory, glory, hallelujah!

Glory, glory, hallelujah!

Our victory is nigh!

Hark! the tumult of the battle; hear the boom of distant guns!

And cries that leap to Heaven, for our loved and
fettered ones!

America is rising for the freedom of her sons,

And ~~The~~ victory is nigh!

CHORUS.

Oh! who shall stay the morning that is bursting from
  the night?

Oh! who shall stay the army that is led by Heaven's
  might?

In brave unbroken column, we shall put our foes to
  flight,

And ~~The~~ victory is nigh!

IN SUNNY LANDS.

In sunny lands I long have strayed,
　　Through valleys wondrous fair;
Where strange, bright flow'rs, in cocoa's shade,
　　Swung on the tropic air.
And happy sound of bird and stream,
　　Wherever I might roam,
Were near, yet sadly would I dream,
　　And pine for sweet, sweet home.

Chorus—

　　Home! home!—dear, happy home!
There's bliss, the purest ~~heart~~ *Earth* can give,
　　In my own dear home!

I've been where wealth and beauty met,
　　And wit, and mirth went round;
And merry feet were tripping light,
　　To sweet, inspiring sound.

Yet, like a lone, imprisoned bird,
   That loves the bright sea foam,
The strain of melody I heard,
   But turned my heart to home!

Oh! not in blooming isles afar,
   The loving soul would roam;
For, where the heart's best treasures are,
   We all may find sweet home.
No marble tow'r may mark the spot—.
   No broad, o'ershad'wing dome—
Mine is a low and humble cot,
   And yet, 'tis sweet, sweet home!

SONG.

The myrtle wraps thy lowly grave
　　In beauty and in bloom;
And bending willows gently wave
　　Their branches o'er thy tomb;
And yet thy own sweet voice I hear,
　　Upon the winds' low sigh;
And feel thy spirit hov'ring near,
　　Too pure and good to die.

Sweet Mary! when the weary world
　　Is sunk in soft repose.
When sunset's banners all are furled,
　　And shadows wrap the rose.
Oh! then but sweeter falls thy tone,
　　Upon my list'ning heart;
Still thou art, as of old, *my own*,
　　And dearer, e'en thou art.

Then wait, my darling! ever sing
   The while I lonely stay;
Oh! let no angel beckoning
   Woo thee, from me away!
Wait till the golden gate shall swing
   Ajar to welcome me,
That I may float, on angel wing,
   To Heaven, led by thee!

ITALIAN CHILD'S SONG.

Swiss Air.

I'm alone, I'm alone, in a drear, foreign land.

   'Tis the voice of the stranger I hear;

And the forms that once sported with me, a gay
     band,

   Are scattered, alas! far and near.

     One dear one sleeps where billows roar

     Their hoarse, wild anthems, evermore;

And the bright pearls rest on his peaceful breast,

   Afar from the land he loved best!

There's a dell, there's a dell where the bright waters
     foamed,

   O'er the gray, mossy rocks, in their way;

And it seems scarce an hour, since I gleefully roamed,

   On its margin, with spirits as gay.

     The silv'ry tone, that cheered me then,

     Is heard no more within the glen;

But the fair, fragile form of my sister is laid

   'Neath the same forest tree where we played.

There's a voice, there's a voice from the pure, spirit
    land.

    Breathing gently its music to me;

And I feel that her spirit is hovering near,

    Though she sleeps far across the blue sea.

      Oh! never, in Italian bow'r,

      Till then had drooped so fair a flow'r;

But I'll weep not, sweet mother, thou now art at
    rest,

    In the bright, sinless land of the blest.

In my dreams, in my dreams, come again the sweet
    days,

    That may never return but in dreams;

And the tears, that ye pity, but brighten my gaze,

    To the bliss of their soft, starry gleams,

      Thus ever sweet my harp shall ring,

      While treasured loves I weep and sing,

Till I sweep, with glad fingers, a new harp of gold,

    With the loved ones, in rapture untold!

COME TO ME ELLA.

Oh! bright is the glow of the deep, starry skies,
    And the sunshine that smiles everywhere;
But dim is their light by the love in thine eyes,
    And the flash of thy soft, sunny hair,
Though costly the pleasures of palaces princely,
    Though Pleasure and Wit meet in many a hall,
Yet give me the cottage where Ella, sweet Ella
    And I dwell in happiness deeper than all.

Chorus—

    Come to me Ella! my own wife Ella!
      Come sit, as of old, on my knee;
    While I clasp to my heart rarer treasures than
      gold—
      An Eden of gladness, and thee!

Around us, all glowing with purple and gold,
    The blossoming meadows are spread;
And roses and lilacs our bower enfold,
    All drooping with fragrance o'erhead.

The bright, cooing birds .build their nest at our
    window,

And fearlessly warble the wealth of their glee;

But sweeter, ah! sweeter, the voice of my Ella,

That whispers in low, cooing love-notes to me!

CHORUS—

    Come to me, Ella! my own wife, Ella!

    Come sit, as of old, on my knee;

    While I clasp to my heart rarer treasures than
        gold—

    An Eden of gladness, and thee!

MINNE-HA-HA.

In the gay, golden summert-ime, long, long ago,
  By the brink of thy bright, laughing stream,
We wandered together, my darling and I,
  In the glow of love's first, happy dream.
The roses were wild that he twined in my hair,
  And lichen grew soft 'neath our tread;
And the white, foaming torrent, and rock where
    it fell,
  Made the chapel wherein we were wed.

CHORUS—

  Oh! wild Minne-ha-ha! thy music was joy,
    And our hearts echoed back all thy song;
  Our Future a dreamland of ecstasy grew,
    And life seemed long—Oh! how long!

  Oh! that sweet gliding summer-time sped like the
      light,
    When the sunset is flaming with gold;
  And darkness and anguish closed 'round me like
      night,
    When my darling lay silent and cold.

There's a sigh in the forest that listened our
vows,
And a wail on the once merry wave;

For the rush of thy torrent he heareth not now,

And thy spray weepeth over his grave.

CHORUS—
Oh! wild Minne-ha-ha! thy music is woe,
And my heart echoes back all thy song,
As I wait for the angels to welcome *me too*—
I wait—I wait—Oh! how long!

Adown in thy valley where violets bloom,

Be, in wildness and tumult, my home;

Let no marble column point out my low tomb,

When the angel, in pity, shall come.

Faithful still, though in death, would I rest by
his side
'Mid the rush and the chant of thy wave;

And the gray, mossy rock, where I knelt as his
bride,
Be the monument over our grave.

CHORUS—
Oh! wild Minne-ha-ha, thy music is woe,
And my heart echoes back all thy song,
As I wait for the angels to welcome me too,
I wait—I wait—Oh! how long!

Oct. 1867.

POOR OLD NANCE, OR "MY DEAR BOY JAMIE'S HAIR."

On Croghan street still stands a cot,
  That sheltered once a dame;
So poor and lonely was her lot,
  None cared to ask her name.
And years went by, and white locks drooped,
  Above her dark eyes glance;
But not a soul yet cared to know
  A word of poor old Nance.

CHORUS—

But oh! her heart was warm and true
  As ever beat for me or you;
And mem'ries bright as earth has known,
  Hung 'round her pathway lone.

One bitter morn she came not forth,
  But pity heeded not;
A week went by, and children missed
  The smoke above her cot:

Their curious eyes her window sought,
    But shrank, and lost their mirth;
For poor old Nance sat, white in death,
    Before her silent hearth!

CHORUS—Yet once her heart, &c.

The tears were frozen on her cheeks;
    Her white lips wore a smile;
Her hands an open Bible pressed,
    With rev'rent touch, the while;
And one bright curl, of sunny gold,
    Lay softly shining there:
And on the time-stained page they read—
    "My dear boy Jamie's hair!"

CHORUS—Oh! yes, her heart, &c.

LOVE'S LAST LULLABY, OR "MAMA SING!"

Summer twilight lost her glow,
   In the pale moon's mellow light.
As a mother, fair and young,
   Watched her babe the lone, still night,
Once, one mocking moment, Death
   Hid the shadow of his wing;
And the dim eyes brightened fair,
   As he whispered, "Mama sing!"

CHORUS—
   By oh! by, my baby by,
   Be thy tears forever dry;
   Rest! my Love! nor wake to weep—
   Rest, baby, rest!   Sleep, baby, sleep!

All her loving labor done,
   She had only now to wait,
Clinging to the pale, sweet one,
   Till he reached the shining gate.

Oh! the agony and love,
　In the kisses gently pressed
On the drooping baby head,
　Pillowed on her aching breast!

By oh! by, my baby by,
Be thy tears forever dry;
Rest, my Love! nor wake to weep—
Rest, baby, rest! Sleep, baby. sleep!

Thus her cadence, soft and sweet
　As an angel's, stirred the air,
While the death shades closed again,
　O'er the eyes that beamed so fair;
Till she hushed him to a sleep,
　Sweeter far than earth's repose—
Waking only on the Breast
　Where a love supernal glows!

By, oh! by, my baby by,
Be thy tears forever dry;
Rest, my Love, nor wake to weep—
Rest, baby, rest! Sleep, baby, sleep!

"SHE SPELT THE PARSON DOWN."

Oh! yes, I'll surely marry,
    At last I've found my girl—
A fair and rosy maiden,
    That sets my heart awhirl.
Her eyes with mirth are brimming,
    Her heart is kind and true;
I more than guess she's willing,
    So I'll marry—would'nt you?

CHORUS—

She's the prettiest little maiden,
    With eyes of brightest brown;
And wise enough, for oh! you know,
    She spelt the parson down!

The moon was brightly beaming,
    The air was soft and cool,
As, on, we slowly wandered,
    Home from the spelling school.

I asked her if she loved me,
And heard her softly say
A word I must not tell you,
But oh! it was not nay.

CHORUS.

Oh! in the bright years coming,
As down life's stream we float,
We'll cast a fond look backwards,
From out our gliding boat;
And lovingly remember
That evening bright and cool,
And bless the time we wandered
Home from the spelling school.

CHORUS.

"ANGELS HOLD HER IN SAFE KEEPING."

IN MEMORY OF LULU—

In the brightness of her beauty,
  We have laid our loved to rest;
We have kissed her waxen forehead,
  And her slender fingers pressed;
While so peaceful was her sleeping,
  And so bright the smile she wore,
That it seemed while yet we lingered,
  That her slumber must be o'er.

CHORUS—

  Gentle Lulu! Darling Lulu!
    Death nor Time shall part our love:
  Soon the angels too will bear me
    To thy blissful home above!

  Lilies, loving hands had scattered,
    Drooped on brow and breast and cheek,
  Breathing, in their silent perfume,
    Sweetest language love can speak;

But their bloom, alas! has withered,
  And their loving breath has fled,
While our lily blooms immortal—
  Darling Lulu is not dead!

CHORUS.

Oft, when fades the sunset glory,
  Comes the voice I love so well;
And her love-smile beams upon me,
  With a calm and holy spell;
Till my yearning soul half pierces,
  Through the shadows cold and gray;
And the breath and glow of Heaven
  Cheer and light my lonely way.

CHORUS.

Then away! with woe and weeping,
  Let my heart her anguish stay!—
Angels hold her in safe keeping,
  Till awakes the coming day,
When her arms shall clasp around me,
  And her kiss be on my brow;
And anew her love hath crowned me
  With a bliss I dream not now!

CONTENTS.

CONTENTS.—CONTINUED.